ABUNDANCE TRIGGERS

How to Shift Yourself Into Prosperity Consciousness Instantly!

KANTA BOSNIAK

illustrations by Kanta Bosniak

Front back and cover photos by Patricia Robin Woodruff. Graphic effects inspired by Carlos A. Gil CD cover graphic of "Abundance Triggers: A Journey of Self-Discovery," by Kanta Bosniak with music by Joshua Bosniak

Copyright © 2011 Kanta Bosniak 2011

All rights reserved. No part of this book may be reproduced or transmitted in any form or by any means, electronic, mechanical, or photographic including photocopying, recording or by any information and retrieval system without written permission of the publisher. No patent liability is assumed with respect to the use of the information contained herein. Although every precaution has been taken in the preparation of this book, the publisher and author assume no liability for errors or omissions. Neither is any liability assumed for damages resulting from the use of this book. The author of this book does not present medical or psychological advice or prescribe the use of any technique to treat medical, or emotional concerns without the advice of an appropriate health professional; either directly or indirectly. The statements herein have not been evaluated by the Food and Drug Administration. This book is intended for the purpose of spiritual growth. In the event that you use any of the information in this book, the author of this book assumes no responsibility for your actions. You assume total responsibility for your actions and their consequences, which may include wholeness, happiness, and joy.

ISBN: 1456502190
ISBN 13: 9781456502195

This book is dedicated to you...

...to you, who want to live your happiest, most productive and prosperous life. May it inspire you to give and receive generously, follow your dreams, and to achieve your highest potential.

May it help you wake up feeling excited to begin your day. And when you may find yourself temporarily swayed by the voice of the sad or angry victim, may it help you shift your state to one of power... reliably, immediately and in the most delightful way!

This book is dedicated to you...

and to my dear friend, Diane Porter Goff

Contents

Dedication iii

Love & Gratitude vii

Preface ix

Introduction xi

Chapter 1: Presence & Awareness 1

Chapter 2: Connection 7

Chapter 3: Happy Memories & Abundance Stories 19

Chapter 4: Desire & Deservingness 51

Chapter 5: The Three Kings: Reframing, Forgiveness & Gratitude 73

Chapter 6: Feeling & Follow-Through: Embodying Joy 79

Chapter 7: Sounds Good 95

Chapter 8: You Who Sit on My Eyelids 101

Chapter 9: Prayer & Meditation 127

Resources 143

Abundance Triggers/Sacred Space Workshops 146

Abundance Triggers, the CD 148

Afterword: Abundance Triggers, the Musical 153

"Each friend represents a world in us, a world possibly not born until they arrive, and it is only by this meeting that a new world is born."
— Anais Nin

Love & Gratitude

Thanks to my friends, family, students, clients, and colleagues for all your encouragement and inspiration. Thanks to Unity Churches, Edgar Cayce's Association for Research and Enlightenment, and Omega Institute, who embraced the workshops related to this book so enthusiastically and have been a support and inspiration to me. Thanks to the workshop participants from around the world. I love meeting you and sharing laughter and creative play together.

Thanks to Heather Rodale, to Revs. Nancy Oristaglio and Steven McClain, to Stacy Castello Hairfield, Lisa Plummer, Joan and Roger Brisson, Diane Porter Goff, Polly Kahl, Emily Stanton, Carlos and Carolyn Gil, Woody and Patricia Robin Woodruff and Louise Devine Loveland.

Thanks to Carly Giesen, Rebecca Bastian, Bethany Bower, Catherine Cummings, Vicky Stata, Rick Allebach, Bruce Jensen, Millicent Greason-Spivak, George Robertson, George Withers, Verna Lisa, Mary Babcock, Sherry Cianciola, Dale Kinley, Melinda Chivian, Kelly Ravel, Robert Radle, and Robert Ryan.

Thanks to Betty Kinley, Joyce Johnson, Kay Turner, Sue Newkirk Niven, Suzi Gablik, Anne Davidson, Jim and Diane Brown, Mark Hodges, Doris Nagle and Theresa Schaeffer, Catherine Stine and Norris Chumley, John and Karen Stine, Betty Zimmer, Hakuin Rose, Joshua and Alicia Bosniak.

And thanks to "You, who sit on my eyelids" and show me beauty in my dreams and everyday life.

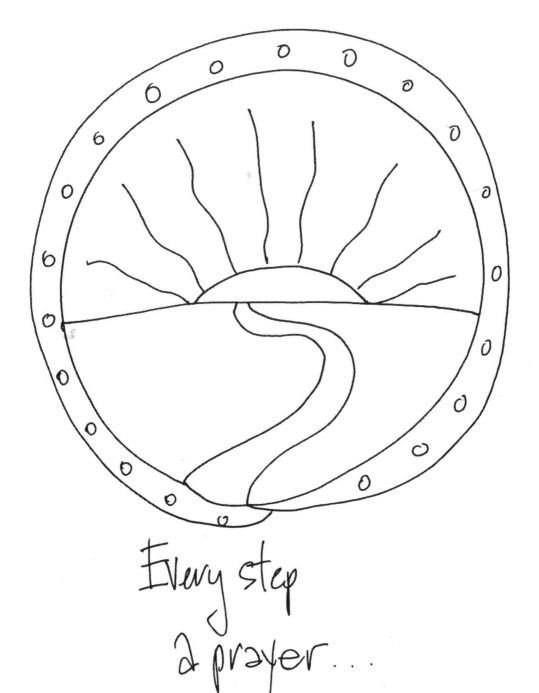

Every step
a prayer....

Preface

by Heather Rodale

As life unfolds, so do unexpected challenges. Whether these challenges are the result of health, relationship, career, care giving or loss, they can sweep us in like a tsunami and encompass every part of our life.

For me, a cancer diagnosis came just after a divorce and a host of additional challenges followed. While trying to find my way out of one huge challenge, I was faced with another.

Abundance Triggers is a wonderful tool box of ideas and inspiration to help regain the quality and vitality of the life we desire. It is not just about "overcoming" the challenges and getting back to our normal life, it may also be about finding our "new normal life" which may be better than the one before.

Just like a road detour, sometimes there are beautiful sites and surprises on the back roads. It may take us longer to reach our destination, or we may even decide we want a different destination. The same is true in life.

Healing begins by the desire to want to get better or resolve the conflict. Then we can explore resources and options that we have not yet practiced or considered.

The key is about trying something new and expanding our "tools" for healing. That is when recovery and rebirth are possible. We will again feel the abundance of the good life we so desire.

It is my pleasure to introduce this book. In it, you will find an enjoyable and engaging process for finding this abundance. In my own healing, creativity was an important component.

Author Kanta Bosniak skillfully weaves information and story, and provides opportunities for creative self-expression as you move through your own renewal.

All Best Wishes,
Heather Rodale
Founder, Healing Through The Arts
www.HTTA.org

Introduction

We hear so much about the importance of thinking positive thoughts. Quantum physicists tell us thought creates our reality, as shamans, medicine men, wise women and priests have taught us for millennia.

OK, we get it. Our bodies respond to chronic emotions by creating chemicals that further habituate these emotions. We form grooves that are hard to jump, and yet jump we must, if we want to begin the task of habituating ourselves to happiness.

But how do we do this? How do we awaken from of the numbness of dulled-down existence to even notice our thoughts, much less direct them? And as we reclaim consciousness, how do we change our living dream experience from semi-nightmare to fully engaged adventure?

There must be tools. And so, there are. My name for them is "abundance triggers." I have made a lifetime study of how to shift thoughts and the emotions they produce to those good feelings, which boost energy and attract wonderful experiences.

Abundance triggers serve to remind you who you really are...like a cosmic string tied around your finger. They remind you that you're loved and they evoke love within you, like pictures of your parent, child or sweetheart. They can take you within, like trance music, or pump you up to clean house, get out the door, and down the road to do the things that are yours to do. They can help you stay on track to do those things.

Of course, it is not the trigger itself that has power to create abundance for you. The trigger is not the worldly abundance you seek, nor is it the state of wholeness and love that you seek on a deeper level.

It's a reminder that you use to snap yourself out of the unpleasant trance of lack and shift yourself into a more resourceful trance: The Alpha State.

That state of joy that athletes, artists, lovers, and meditators know so well. And so do you, in flashes, moments, in peak experiences and periods of relative peace.

Perhaps you'd like to stretch those moments into how your life simply IS? To let that pleasure expand so that you ***stay*** grounded, confident, motivated, willing to receive and enjoy your good? So that you create a new "default state," habituating yourself to happiness?

You have that power. You are the one who chooses to use the trigger. You create the "button," you push it and you allow it to work...by connecting you with your Source, that power we find it convenient to call God.

In the jargon of Hypnosis, abundance triggers might be termed "anchors" or "post-hypnotic suggestions" that you use for yourself. Let's look abundance triggers, for a moment, as a form of self-hypnosis.

When This Happens, That Happens

An "anchor" is a positive trigger. It's used to interrupt a pattern and to imbed a more resourceful one. "Post-hypnotic suggestion" connects an anchor with a desired behavior. It works like this: When something happens, something else follows.

When I see (hear, touch feel) _____ I feel (or do) _____.

Ex. When the sun comes up, I awaken, feeling great.

You've probably seen funky old movies which depict post-hypnotic suggestion as a tool for mind-control. A Svengali-like hypnotist whispers something like "pomegranate" into the telephone and the guy on the other end of the line goes wonky and robs a bank. Hypnosis doesn't work like that. It's teamwork. Your team works together to achieve your goal.

How Self-Hypnosis Works

Introducing "Team You," a distinguished crew, indeed: Your conscious mind, your subconscious mind, and God. The fourth member may be a coach/hypnotist or you can serve this function for yourself. It takes a little more work, but I'll help you learn how to do it. That's what I do! And the benefits are huge. Teach yourself to fish, and you'll eat well for life.

Hypnosis is truly guided meditation...full-tilt, highly focused prayer. You ask, and are willing and God does the heavy lifting! Self- hypnosis works similarly, without the hypnotist as part of the equation. What does the hypnotist do and how can you do it on your own with this book?

The hypnotist acts as a spiritual coach to help you clarify your goals, your strongest motivations, and identify your most effective anchors. S/he also helps you move into that natural state of harmonious relaxation in which your parts work cohesively.

This book will help you coach and relax yourself and get all your wheels going in the same direction: Happiness. And more than that, it will help you develop the ability to manage your state...to be happy anytime you choose. How do you begin and what do you do?

Pushing the "Happy" Button

In a relaxed and focused moment, you make an agreement with yourself that you will use a certain stimulus to trigger a state of well-being, from which you will naturally and easily attract abundance. Sort of like pushing the "Happy" button. The trigger can be anything you like. And you can create as many triggers as you like.

This book will guide you through the creation and use of these abundance triggers. It will also show you techniques to stop negative thinking at its roots, so that you claim back your power to maintain your well-being. As you habituate the Happy Button the Not-So-Happy one atrophies from sheer lack of use, and joy becomes, more and more, your baseline state.

This phenomenon is explained quite beautifully in more scientific terms in the section on receptors in the documentary film, **What the Bleep Do We Know?**, as well as in the metaphor of the two dogs. You know the one I mean. Two dogs come to your door every day begging for food, a mean one and a friendly one. Which one grows stronger? The one you feed. Abundance triggers nourish your friendly pup, which loves you unconditionally, and loves to play!

How I Discovered Abundance Triggers

So you know that the offerings in this book are not merely theoretical Pollyannaisms, I'll share with you that life has given me plenty of grist for the learning mill.

I began consciously developing abundance triggers for myself at the age of five, in response to physical, emotional and sexual abuse. My home was presided over by an alcoholic father, who molested me and a paranoid schizophrenic mother, who singled me out from my other two siblings as the main target for her projected shame and rage.

As I began kindergarten and needed to navigate the world, the pain became so overwhelming that to endure it I developed techniques to shift my state.

I learned to induce alpha states in a variety of ways: by breathing, in silence and song, in nature, in physical activity and creative expression. I got out of my mother's way into the safety of the neighborhood on my bike and enjoyed the feeling of movement and the flow of air on my face and body. I did eyes-open meditation by gazing at the faces of flowers and breathing in their scents.

I lay underneath the piano when my father played Rachmaninoff, Chopin, Lionel Hampton and Hoagy Carmichael. I let the sound transport me into sweet awareness and appreciation.

I hiked alone through woods, and plugged into the healing peace and majesty of the forest. Sometimes I took a trowel and earthen bowl, dug up mosses and small plants and created my own magical mini-worlds to adorn the arrangements of treasured objects atop my bureau...my first altar art.

I holed up in my room and drew or read or made up stories with my dolls. I sketched images of the mother I wanted, a Mother who would love me without condition and with whom I would feel safe and worthy.

I drew circular drawings I now know as mandalas. They eased my anxiety and made me feel whole. I discovered joy in singing and dancing. As soon as I could read, I sopped up fables and fairy tales. Teaching stories like **The Little Engine that Could** were my soul food. Later, I moved on to myths and biographies of inspiring people.

I learned the power of affirmation to create new stories and new realities for myself and others...I and began to write my own. I nourished self-empathy and self-expression with journaling, and fell in love with films.

I continued to develop strengths with each stage and age of life. I made a decision at seventeen to become a happy person, whatever it would take, and to share what I learned. That decision launched a learning quest which has been juicy and exciting. And though it included the ups and downs of life, it's been progressively free of inner drama.

I overcame alcohol abuse, survived cancer, worked through the loss of loved ones and financial assets, and extricated myself from a marriage that turned emotionally abusive. I faced many of the tests of life that you may have faced or may be dealing with right now, as we do, in some form or another.

I came to think of these challenges as art supplies for creating my most beautiful and meaningful life. A "miracle" experienced at twenty (which I share in this book), captured my attention and held it fast and forever.

It deeply anchored the understanding that every challenge offers a gift. From that point on, my eagerness and curiosity to discover those gifts began to outweigh my fear of engaging. ***"I think I can"*** had long ago become my mantra and so, I could.

"Miracles" kept happening, and I kept thriving and prospering! You can read some pretty wild ones in Chapter 3. Each challenge became easier, because I could manage my state better and better. I learned how to keep my focus on what's real. I replaced the yearning for approval of "the other" with genuine delight in my own company and belief in myself.

I learned that loss is temporary and illusory. And love is forever. I put the sad, angry, fearful ego on a diet. I fed it less self-pity, and more compassion. Over time and with the use of abundance triggers, it lost power and I gained Presence.

I became the happy person my seventeen year old self had promised I would be, and my Higher Self helped me become. And I became a more and more skillful conscious creator. This is our birthright and our curriculum as humans.

The seed techniques outlined in this book germinated, grew, and blossomed in a garden which I now realize is eternal, common to us all, and meant to universally be shared. Teaching them has been my passion throughout my life, as artist, writer, spiritual coach, and creator of Guided Meditations.

Quantabulous You!

We all share a common Oneness and a common tendency to resist and deny our natural state of bliss. Judgment and self-criticism are the adversaries. And, as in all good Hero's Journeys, these adversaries are the secret allies we use to hone and own our strengths as spiritual warriors.

Each and every one of us must find ways to master our negative mind. It is our personal challenge, our collective responsibility as citizens of the earth, and our spiritual destiny. To truly heal we must be willing to feel.

Abundance Triggers

We must awaken from the negative trances we keep in place with mean and meaningless television, prescription drugs, overindulgent torpor, self-critical mind-static, and co-dependent relationships and choose more resourceful trances!

As we discover ways to connect with the healer and lover within, we learn to accept our own magnificence. We learn to be the masters of self-directed positive focus we were always meant to be, triggering abundance for ourselves and our world.

You already have developed some skills for managing your state, for giving and receiving. In this book, you will find information, stories, practical tips, visualizations and creative journal exercises to strengthen and expand these talents and abilities. In building your own skills for abundant living, you bless your family, friends and all of us. Thank you!

Please feel free to shut off your censor with the writing and drawing exercises and be as silly and spontaneous as you like. It's not about "good writing" or "great art"; it's all about play!

It is my hope and my intention that this book will help you make lasting change and that it will continue to be a valuable resource for you to as you move forward.

When I hear, as I often do, from readers and listeners, that just seeing my books and CDs them on their bedside table is a state-shifter, I feel happy, because that has always been my intention.

It's made to inspire you with content, the process it offers for you, and if you own it in hard-copy form, as a three- dimensional visual anchor for joy that you can place in your home to remind yourself how wonderful you really are!

Even if you have purchased it as a download, your takeaway is still both process and product.

Because the journal that you will create for yourself as you write, draw and imagine will provide you with **_an instant go-to_** for your own personalized abundance triggers!

I encourage you, even after you complete the Abundance Triggers exercises, to continue using the journal in which you did those exercises as a daily Gratitude Journal.

Recording your successes, synchronicities, blessings and shifts will continue to build your attracting power, making you the irresistible force of nature you were always meant to be.

You may want to use a scrapbook-type binding for your journal, so that you can easily incorporate photos and mementos.

May you connect with the prospering spirit within you, enjoy the richness and sweetness of life and may your cup run over with...

Abundant Blessings,

Kanta ♡

"Something opens our wings.
Something makes boredom
and hurt disappear.
Someone fills the cup
in front of us.
We taste only sacredness."

—Rumi

Chapter 1

Presence & Awareness

Basic Toolbox

This chapter will offer you some simple quick and reliable ways to feel good. They're not sexy or complicated. You could think of them as spiritual first aids or as basic tools for your state-shifting kit. If you start with a screwdriver, pliers, a wrench and a hammer, there's a lot you can do. And what sort of tool box wouldn't include them?

Later, we can add some fancy stuff. If you want a taste of the truly amazing abundance you're capable of, you can go ahead and peek at the stories chapter. Or save it for when you get there, and enjoy your process as it unfolds. And for now, let's get started...

Now

The most immediate way to feel shift your state is to bring yourself into here and now, and into your body. Focusing on your physical sensations will help you do this.

1. What do you see? Hear? Feel? Look without having to assign meaning. Just notice the shapes and colors. Let yourself experience sounds without needing to listen or interpret the sounds. Let them wash over you.

    Your skin is your largest organ and, except for the hair on your head, it defines the outer edges of your body. Let yourself take a moment to feel your skin...the feeling of the air on your face, your hands... anyplace where the air caresses your body.

Tune into the sensations of your body coverings, your clothes and shoes...if you're reading in bed your nightclothes, the sheets...the gentle weight of the blankets. Feel your body coverings as a kind of cocoon, a cozy protective layer that embraces you.

Ground and Breathe

We all have an energetic body. When we feel stressed, our energy can get squeezed up into our heads. Sometimes it might feel like it's hovering a little above your head, almost as if the energetic body, feeling unsafe, is trying to flee the physical body. Or you might have a swirling sensation. The simple solution that provides relief is to ground yourself.

2. Take your attention up to the top of your head and imagine moving it down into your body, by gently redirecting your focus of attention, into your head, your neck, down into your chest, and all the way down into your belly.

   If you are standing, focus on the contact of your feet with the floor. If you are sitting, feel your feet on the floor and your buttocks on the chair. If you are lying down on your back (great for grounding) focus on the contact the entire back of your body has with the floor.

   Let your body feel the way it is supported and rest a few moments, taking nice deep breaths as you focus on your lower abdomen.

Move It!

We're made to move. If we stay sedentary for hours on end, our energy can get "backed up," which can result in feeling either antsy or lethargic. To get the energy flowing again:

3. Take a brisk walk.

4. If you're working on the computer (at home or in an office with a door that closes) try a few minutes of stretches.

5. Take a dance break!

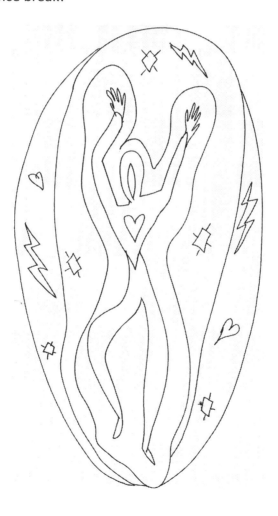

Water: Think and Drink Love

Studies have shown that proper hydration improves mood. Dr. Masaru Emoto also proved in his research that positive words like "Love and Gratitude" actually make beneficial changes in water molecules.

His book "The Hidden Messages in Water" gives you a taste of some of the science and beauty of this. In it can you see pictures of what happens to water when it's exposed to negative or positive thoughts and words.

Watery abundance triggers:

6. Bless your water.

7. Speak kind words to yourself and others. Your body is mostly made of water, and it responds to every word and thought.

8. Play with water! Write a keyword or phrase, like "Peace and Prosperity," "Love and Gratitude," "Healing," "Release," or "Hope" on a piece of paper and place a filled glass of drinking glass on it for an hour or so. Then, enjoy!

Orange You Glad

Scientists and aromatherapists agree that citrus has a mood-lifting effect. It's refreshing, optimistic and, well, happy. Probably why Clinique's "Happy" fragrance is reminiscent of a Creamsicle (and I mean that in a good way)! "Cheerful" orange teams up with "warm and loving" vanilla. Mmm!

Fragrance can be an instant and very powerful way to trigger a state of well-being. So can taste. I used to play field hockey as a teen. Miss Richardson, our red-headed Scottish coach, gave us cut-up oranges to boost our energy mid-game. Worked every time.

9. Add a wedge of lemon to your water.

10. Squeeze some lime on your taco salad.

11. Take a whiff of sweet orange essential oil or dab it on your wrists for all day optimism.

Left, Right, Shift!

Many of us stay in our left brain for long periods of time. This can be very stressful. For a quick boost to your mood and productivity:

Abundance Triggers

12. Let your mind rest and move into the creative, imaginative Right Brain. Take few deep breaths, look out the widow, step away from your desk, have a glass of water, or daydream!

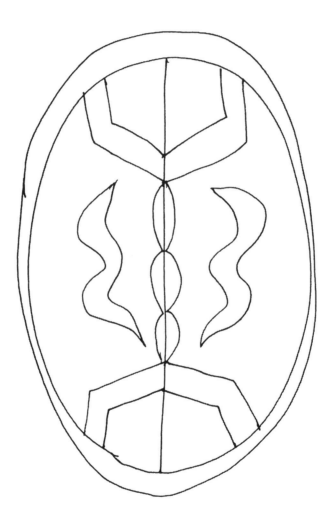

Chapter 2

Connection

Feeling Like "Yourself"...

Now let's create some customized triggers for you. We'll identify and list what's most fun, relaxing, and inspiring for you and establish some intentions to excite and sustain you. You can use this list as an abundance trigger buffet, for when you need soul nourishment.

When we shift ourselves back into a state of relaxed well-being, we may describe it this way: "I'm feeling like myself again." I invite you to consider what that means, so that you can "feel like yourself" at will. What does it mean to "feel like you"? Who is the "you" that has these preferences? And why are your preferences important?

You are a unique Expression of Divinity in You as You, that's why!

Your Playful Self & The Cosmic GPS

"It is the childlike mind that finds the Kingdom"
-Charles Fillmore

We each have unique lessons to learn, qualities to develop, and our own path to walk. Our sensors go off when we veer off our path. The guidance system is simple. "Course correction" message: you get the blahs. "You're on track" message: you get the yippees! You feel good, inspired, and happy...and like a little kid, energized and playful. Play is as essential as rest. And, it helps you generate the excitement that attracts the flow of abundance! That's why it's so important to remember to have fun. The next section will help with this.

Your Short List

Let's start by making a resource list, a sort of short list of what you love, what you most enjoy and what you most appreciate…those state-shifting things that when you do them, you feel good. List as many as you like in your journal, leaving a little space for later additions that may occur to you.

Please be as specific and as generous as you can. Do you prefer green tea? Dark roast coffee? A nice hot shower or a bubble bath?

Roller skating at the park? Lolling on the beach? Burrowing under a squishy comforter with a novel? Goodwill hunting? Is the perfume counter at Macy's your instant pick-me-up? All of the above?

Relaxation and Fun

1. What feels deliciously relaxing for you?

2. What makes you feel cozy and comfy?

3. What makes you feel warm and loving?

4. What's fun for you?

5. What revs you up?

6. What gives you pleasure?

7. What makes you laugh?

8. What makes you feel beautiful or handsome?

9. What physical activities do you enjoy?

10. List your favorite places to visit (or places you'd like to go), that you could get to within fifteen minutes… thirty minutes…an hour…a day…a weekend.

11. How do express your creativity?

12. Refer to your Short List anytime you want to nudge yourself into a better-feeling place.

Tales of Brave Ulysses, My Precious

Mythic stories, as Joseph Campbell said, have one foot in human life and one in transcendence. They show the hero overcoming human challenges and point the way to our inner hero, from the unconscious illusion of separation to union with the Divine.

The ego's siren song tries to seduce us into the rocky water of self-pity and to reaching out for poor substitutes for bliss: empty sex, needy love, substances and behaviors that can never satisfy.

We hear that voice, cloyingly sweet and yet creepy, as if the Gollum were calling out to your self-pity, "My Precioussss"…trying to persuade you that you are alone, fallen out of the universe, friendless, Godless and forgotten, on a no-exit, random planet.

That song has the most power when we hear it unconsciously. Listen to it directly, and its dissonance is apparent. Look it in the face, and its ugliness emerges. Allow yourself to accurately sense its agenda, and you navigate safely past Isolation Island and into more peaceful waters.

There's a place for therapy, support groups, mentorship and temporarily uneven friendship…those times when we reach out to someone else to hold the truth of who we are. We may be at a place on our path when we do not yet have the strength to do it for ourselves. Or we may find ourselves in a situation so immediately challenging that we need help to find our ground.

And we are all moving toward spiritual mastery. Ultimately we learn to take responsibility for our own happiness. On this journey, we find ourselves on a new road (or least, new to us. It's a road that every master has traveled).

> *"People rarely succeed unless they have fun in what they are doing."*
> -Dale Carnegie

Commitment to Happiness: Paradigm and Paradox

Most of us have dreams and goals for what we want to accomplish in our lives. The old paradigm focuses on achievements and possessions as end product. Certificates on the wall and in the bank, the trophy wife or husband...stuff.

Don't get me wrong. Stuff is fun. I like stuff, and money is a convenient commodity. And so are the more abstract versions of stuff: career success, respect and recognition, loving relationships.

Here's the paradox: Joy and en-joy are connected. It's not about the stuff; it's about learning to be in joy and love. We don't take the stuff or the people with us; we take what we learned about joy and love.

And yet the more we cultivate joy and love, the more we attract the stuff that we can en-joy in human life. It doesn't last and it doesn't matter...and yet it's fun. And that's great!

13. What does happiness feel like in your body?

14. Write a letter of 100% commitment to your happiness, starting right now. Sign and date it.

15. Tune into your Higher Self, the highest, wisest part of you. Feel the love and support. Now, write a letter from your Higher Self to you stating of 100% commitment to your happiness, starting right now. Sign ("Sincerely, Your Higher Self") and date it, put it in an envelope, and send it to yourself in the mail.

Inside Job

*"Seek ye first the Kingdom of God and
all these things will be added to you."*
-Jesus

We learn to go within for connection, find the love and approval there. Then, miracles happen. The heart opens and is filled to overflowing. When we reach out it is not to hold, hoard, or take hostages in relationship, but to share, enjoy and extend love.

As our ears become more and more attuned to the music of love, we become less tolerant of low-level mind static. We become aware of the noise, and take the time to adjust the dial for clear connection.

Babies learn love from their mother's response. Their cry signals need and the need is met. Mature relationship is not self-seeking nor is it mutual medication. It's delight, joy, play. On our spiritual learning curve, we gradually move away from demanding love from the outside as a knee-jerk response to the whimpering cry of ego.

We learn to self-soothe. We eventually learn to connect **first** with Source. And we learn to create our own abundance triggers for connection. Here is a three-step process that you can use as a state-shifter.

Three Times a Lover

16. Remember first that you ARE Love. You ARE Source expressed as you. Next, remember that you are loved by Source and by your mentors in spirit. You are surrounded by Love! When you feel better, then reach out.

    Your call to the "other" will be in integrity. And it will support and nourish mature relationship and anchor the habit of happy connection.

17. List any non-physical support whose presence you feel or would like to feel...Higher Power, Higher Self, Teachers, Guides & Angels.

18. Spiritual Support Mandala: Draw a picture of yourself encircled by your spiritual supporters, showing them sending love and positive energy to you.

19. Draw a picture of yourself standing in a lush garden. Draw the roots of the flowers and plants on the soil's surface. Draw big, strong roots coming out from the bottoms of your feet, and penetrating deeply into the soil.

20. List twelve loved ones, living or in spirit. Include family, friends, or anyone with whom you feel a close connection.

21. For each entry, write a sentence or so about what you most appreciate about the person.

22. For each entry, imagine that you are that person and write a sentence or so of appreciation for you from his or her perspective.

23. Place pictures of your loved ones where you can see them every day.

24. "Circle of Love" Collage Mandala: Draw a circle in your journal, on a piece of poster board or other surface. Collect a "headshot" photo of yourself, and one each of the twelve friends and loved ones. Make color copies, reducing sizes to fit your chosen framework.

Put yourself in the center and arrange the others around you, as you like. Paste them in and embellish with colored pencils, markers, paint, whatever pleases you. If you have been working on wood, glaze your creation and back with a saw tooth hanger.

25. Reach out. Make a call, send an email, or visit someone you love. Put yourself on a no whining, no criticism diet.

26. Appreciate what you have. Appreciate yourself and others.

27. Put words to your appreciation. Give thanks and praise. What do you enjoy most about your life right now?

28. Whom do you admire?

29. What do you admire about yourself? (Note: you will have a chance to visit this question again; it's *that* important that you love you!)

Give Back

30. Tithe. Give back to Spirit by supporting the channels through which you receive it (be that channel your church, or your hairdresser...).

31. Who or what nurtures you spiritually? How can you give of your time, talent and/or financial support?

32. Contribute. Give back to your community. Service is one of the most powerful abundance triggers of all!

33. What sort of service do you enjoy (or think you might enjoy)?

34. Lean into life. Give back to your inner guidance by following its promptings to action.

35. What do you feel most inspired to do? (If you don't know, take a wild guess.)

It's Your Thing

36. What is the juiciest dream you have for yourself?

37. What would this look like, sound like feel like? How will you know that you have achieved it?

38. Write a letter of intention to yourself to make this real. Sign and date it.

39. Write a letter to God asking for help with making this real. Sign and date it.

40. Take steps every day and record them in your journal

41. Notice and appreciate your progress.

42. Notice and give thanks for the help that shows up for you.

From Nervous to Service

*Then you will come to walk cheerfully over the
world, answering that of God in everyone."
- George Fox*

Doing your thing in the world may not seem like a "give back." And I invite you to begin thinking of it as one. Because it will remove self-consciousness, shame and fear. It will move you from thinking of what you do as a performance that will be judged… and into thinking of it as a gift that flows through you.

This removes the burden of trying to force things or to control people or events. That's the job of your Higher Power. As you keep in contact through prayer and meditation, you will know the steps to take in just the right timing for you.

Evening and Morning Meditations

43. Evening: Take a few moments in the evening to give thanks for the day. Appreciate your accomplishments. Observe any mistakes you may have made. How might you have chosen to do things differently? If you have amends to make to yourself or others, resolve to do that. Now forgive the mistakes. Their purpose was learning and you did that. Ask for guidance in your sleep.

Abundance Triggers

44. Morning: In the morning, before you arise, retrieve whatever guidance you may have received. Give thanks for that guidance, and for your life. Send love into the day…to the people you will encounter and the places you'll go. Remember to send love along to yourself, as you imagine yourself moving through the day. Imagine and describe a happy and productive day. Give thanks in advance and offer a Namaste to God and all creation.

Bubble Up!

45. Visualization: Surround yourself with a bubble of love and light before you leave the house each day. Inside your bubble, you can stay happy and relaxed, regardless of what's going on around you.

NAMASTE

I honor the place in you where Spirit lives. I honor the place in you which is of Love, of Truth, of Light, of Peace. When you are in that place in you and I am in that place in me, we are One.

Chapter 3

Happy Memories & Abundance Stories

Draw on Positive Memories

One of the best abundance triggers is your own memory of past success.

Even stories **about** stories can quiet fear, by shining light on it. I once had the extreme pleasure of experiencing "An Evening with Rumi" presented by poet and translator Coleman Barks and friends. Barks interpreted the master's tale about a cow. He was accompanied by some musicians and a dancer, who performed the part of the hapless bovine.

Every day, the story went; this cow would graze on green grasses and plentiful grains in sunny fields. By day, she became fat and sassy. At night, she could not see the sun, the fields. She panicked, and worried herself skinny. Each day she ate and rejoiced. Each night she lost her gains in fear and stress.

Failing to hold in her mind the memory of the sun, its once and future gifts, or the constancy of its rhythms, she stayed on a treadmill of giddy delight and deep despair. This is a cow who needs an abundance trigger! If only she could remember…

Memory can be a tool for faith. Recalling evidence of love working in our life can awaken us from the shady nightmares of doubt into sunny clarity. I'm going to share a few stories from my own life and a couple clients have shared with me. Each of these demonstrates the workings of Divine providence and answered prayer. Sometimes this "prayer" was fervent and repeated from a deep place of desire. Sometimes it was but a passing thought, lighter than air.

Always it was genuine, heartfelt and offered with a sense of trust. And that's what matters most, for answered prayer: **trust**. I hope that these stories will inspire you to recall... and to create... some stories of your own.

Prayers can be quite literal responses to exactly what you ask for...and much more! Demonstrations of this principle weave through many of these stories.

Another common thread is this: We often learn by contrast. When we have a powerful "don't want" that makes us aware of what we want, and we're willing to receive it, and feel confident that it will, it must inevitably show up. Often, it comes remarkably quickly!

Meditation Class "Miracle"

I began doing Guided Imagery as a Penn student, living off campus in West Philadelphia. I had meditated in some form or another for fifteen of my twenty years and already had some interesting spiritual experiences under my belt. I was so excited to be exposed to new ideas and to learn.

I attended a lecture by the Zen author Alan Watts. In addition to his books I devoured **Autobiography of a Yogi**, Edgar Cayce, Ram Dass, and books by the founder of Ananda Marga Yoga Society, P.R. Sarkar, affectionately known as Baba.

I wasn't much of a guru person or a rule follower and I didn't necessarily agree with all his writings. I thought, if I ever met Baba, he would hardly approve of my independent thinking. But I didn't let this stop me. I loved the meditation and the philosophy, pursued certification as a Meditation Teacher and after a period of study, was given the go-ahead.

We taught in pairs, which could be described as Mind/Body dyads. One taught the philosophy and practice of Meditation and facilitated a Guided Meditation. The other instructed the class in Hatha Yoga postures. Though I could and did do both, after a while I found my right niche as the Meditation half of the spiritual pizza pie. My usual teaching venues were Albert Einstein Hospital, University and Center City groups.

One day, I got a call from one of the Philadelphia yoga teachers. The female half of a couple who taught a class at Graterford Prison had fallen ill. Her partner, whom I'll call Joe taught Hatha Yoga and needed a substitute Meditation teacher. Graterford is a maximum security prison for men. Men who have done really bad things.

To this day, I don't know why I said I'd do it. I'm not fond of confined spaces. I love my freedom and my favorite place is the open highway. I didn't like Joe much. I found his energy unpleasant and invasive.

I hadn't even begun my survivor recovery and was extra-sensitive to iffy boundaries. So, the idea of spending two hours in a car with him and an hour and a half teaching in such an intense environment was daunting.

The ride was indeed more than a bit uncomfortable for me. Joe was chatty; I wanted quiet to focus and ground myself. I arrived tense but determined to do a good job. It got worse, of course! I was a blonde haired Barbie in a house of incarcerated men, looking through the bars at us, whistling, ogling, and yelling words I tried not to hear.

I began saying an inner prayer to screen them out, keep myself focused, and keep my fear and judgment at bay. "Please God," I said, "Help me find a way to remember that these men are spiritual beings. Help me see them with respect. Help me do my job."

As we were escorted further and further into the bowels of the building, we had to pass through several security gates. Steel cage-like doors slid open to let us through and slid shut behind us. I kept silently saying that prayer, "Give me a way to remember that they're spiritual beings. Help me see them with respect. Help me do my job."

We were guided down the staircase that led to the classroom. Apparently, the previous class had just ended. As we descended, prisoners were coming ascending the same set of stairs. Big, tall, scary-looking guys, way too close for any semblance of comfort.

I continued to repeat my prayer as we entered the room and the students filed in behind us and took their places. Joe and I sat on the floor in the front of the room, facing two dozen men or so, also sitting cross-legged.

I closed my eyes and said my prayer one more time...and trusted.

When I opened my eyes, I saw beautiful lights around each one of those men. Some of the lights were white, some were golden-white. Some were greenish. Some were various tones of blue: teal, indigo, and cobalt. I had never seen anything like that before. It was the first time I saw auras, and I will never forget it.

My prayer had been answered. I saw them as spiritual beings, with respect, and I was able to do my job better than I had ever done it before.

1. Describe a time when you were able to see someone with new eyes of compassion and respect.

2. What words, ideas or images might you use to remind yourself that the people you interact with are spiritual beings?

Triple Whammy

It was a week before Christmas. I was a young wife and mother, living in Virginia in the foothills of the Blue Ridge Mountains. My husband was at work. Our little boy was at school. And I was having a pity party. I sat alone in our rustic cabin in a woodsy hollow, taking time out from my artistic endeavors to mope.

We were rich in land, and rich in beauty. I had continued my meditation practice. I became deeply involved in the recovery community and had been working my early life survivor and ACOA issues with a therapist. I was reading books by recovery and personal growth writers John Bradshaw, Janet Woititz, and Harville Hendrix.

I'd also been also studying New Thought philosophy for some time now. More books! I read Catherine Ponder, Shakti Gawain, Arnold Patent and more.

Thought creates. I got it intellectually and had been working on directing my thoughts, with some success, since all the way back to my yogi days. And as before, I was teaching spiritual growth classes with a teaching partner.

And yet, in this moment, I felt sad, deprived. That all too familiar "poor me" feeling had slipped in the door while I wasn't looking. As I told myself a story about motherlessness, I slid even further. I was a sad and resentful ten year old now. Other people - "normal" people from "normal" families - would see their mothers on Christmas. Their mothers would be delighted to see them. Would hug them, smile at them, would give them a token of love in the form of a gift. But not me.

I was estranged from my mentally ill mother. Her terrifying physical abuse had ended around my fifteenth birthday, when I was big and strong enough to hit her back. I did just that in a watershed moment.

But the violence had taken a heavy toll. I struggled with post traumatic stress. It would be many years until I stopped being afraid. Until my startle reflex would subside. Until I stopped having nightmares. And the emotional and verbal abuse only ended when, to preserve my sanity and create the emotional safety I needed for recovery, I severed contact with her.

I felt yearning both as a daughter and as a mother. I wished I could provide more for my son. The yearning generalized and expanded as yearning does, once you get started. My siblings were wealthy by comparison (oh, how the ego loves comparison!)...

...this friend owned seventy-eight acres, that one ninety-nine...I could barely afford the modest gifts I'd bought for family and close friends, and felt sad and resentful that there was no money left for a gift for myself. What about me?

And then, for whatever reason, my ruminations came to a sudden stop. It was my Light Bulb Moment.

Money had never been important to me! So, of course I didn't have it. I had grown up with it; I had taken it for granted. And frankly, I didn't respect it all that much.

What had been important to me was my survivor and ACOA recovery. I had invested my time and energy in my spiritual recovery life. That I had come from such abuse and dysfunction and was alive and sane was in and of itself an accomplishment. I had a family that I loved and wonderful friends. I lived in beauty. I was actually becoming a happy person. That's abundance!

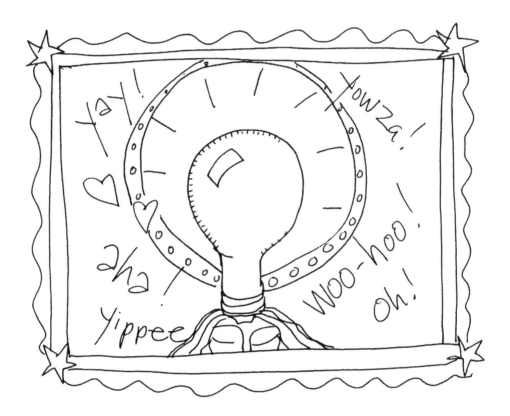

In that moment, I took responsibility for my own creation. I appreciated the fact that my priorities had been, for me, correct. Spirituality has been and always will be always be my first love. And my recovery had permitted me to keep myself intact and able now to consider moving beyond the barest survival level.

I realized that if I wanted to have money now that I might consider this as an option that was open to me. I also felt appreciation and gratitude for my recovery. I had found "mother" (love, acceptance and soul nourishment) in God.

I released my sadness about mother with a little "m" and celebrated my appreciation for Mother with a big "M." That energy we call God, Holy Spirit, Universe, Christ Consciousness, Mother, Father, Mother/Father, Source…would respond to my desire to create in this exciting new area. My practical prayers would be responded to just as my spiritual ones had been. I began to realize that exploring prosperity could be part of my recovery and spiritual life! A part that up until now, I had neglected.

BAM! It was a shift so profound, I felt it physically as a wave of happiness and joy in my heart center and in the back of my head, close to the nape of the neck.

I made up a mantra for myself to affirm that "Mother" was in my life as God and that God and I were prosperity partners: "My Mother loves, nourishes and supports me in every way, including financially." Another wave of good feeling. I was on a roll!

I decided to celebrate. I gave a party, right then and there. When I was a little kid, I used to give fancy tea parties for my teddy bears and dolls. This day, I did the grown up version for me, myself, and God. I began making myself a cup of fresh ground coffee.

And then, the coffee maker broke. Mr. Coffee died a horrible and very messy death. Dark steaming liquid streamed all over my counter and ran down the hand-stenciled wooden cabinet. As I cleaned it up, my heart sank…for just a few seconds. I knew I didn't have the money to replace the machine. Not now…but wait…

My Mother loves nourishes and supports me, I thought. *And the Universe will bring me another coffeemaker. I don't know how or when, but I know it'll happen.*

And then, I added a bit of real chutzpah! *And since I'm asking, I'd like a Pause 'n' Serve model, please!* They're pretty much standard now, but in the mid eighties they were cool and new and I figured, *if I'm asking, I should ask for what I really want!*

And then, I turned it over and forgot about it. I reached back deep into the cabinet, excavated my Melita single cup ceramic cone, boiled some water, and made a cup of yummy brew. There's always a way to enjoy right now!

A few days later, I was on my way to the car, where my husband Murray and son Joshua were waiting. I hurriedly slung my black leather handbag over my shoulder…and the strap broke.

This time, I did even better. In a flash, I passed through the ironic observation that I was going to the fashion capital of the world with a broken purse. And then, I moved into excitement. I was getting to practice my affirmation again!

My Mother loves, nourishes and supports me in every way, including financially, and the Universe will bring me another black leather handbag. I don't know how or when but I know it'll happen.

I got in the car, decided to enjoy the trip broken purse and all, and started doing so, immediately.

We arrived at my brother John's house in suburban Philadelphia. No sooner did I cross the threshold than my sister-in-law Karen asked, "Kanta, do you need a coffeemaker? Because I won one in a raffle, and I already have a coffeemaker. I offered it to your mother…and she said she didn't need it either. It's still in the box on the floor if the dining room closet."

And there it was, in a box marked "Pause 'n' Serve." Well, that got my attention!

We enjoyed a wonderful visit with my brother's family and then a great visit with my sister's family in New York City. On our way back through Philly, we spent one more night at John's.

As we loaded our suitcases in the back of the car the next morning, Karen said, "Kanta, could you use a black leather handbag? Because I won one in a raffle, the same raffle at the same event, and I don't need it. It's yours if you like it."

It was gorgeous! Soft, beautiful leather, classic design. It looked like something I would have picked out for myself if I had a couple hundred dollars to spend at Lord & Taylor's. What was even more stunning was the speed and specificity of my answered prayer. And that wasn't all.

Two weeks after we arrived at home, John called me up. "I don't know how I could have forgotten," he said. "But Mom gave me something for you. I think it's money. I'll put it in the mail to you first thing tomorrow morning."

It was money. It was a money order for a thousand dollars, with a note. An oddly written one, to be sure. And yet, in it, she wished me well. I realized that she loved me as best she could. That she was trying to make amends.

I was grateful that she had opened the lines of communication once again and I was willing to respond and see what would happen. At the very least, regardless of the outcome, it was nice to know that she cared. That was, and still is, a gift beyond measure.

My mantra had permanently anchored itself in physical reality and in my psyche as an abundance trigger. *My Mother loves nourishes and supports me in every way, including financially.*

I used the handbag for two or three years. When I retired it, I cut the leather into pieces that I incorporated into a long, wearable art vest, which I still wear sometimes. The vest itself has become an abundance trigger for me.

And as if this weren't already an amazing enough demonstration, consider this: My sister-in-law won her raffle prizes **before** my coffeemaker and pocketbook broke!

Not only had my spiritual Source given me the things I needed and the opportunity to re-explore my relationship with my mother, but I had been given the most precious of gift of all: soul food.

I received insights into the manifestation process, realization that sequential time is purely a limited human concept…the understanding that our gifts are on the way to us before we even know we need them. Holy Wow!

As a mother notices and nourishes budding talents in her child, so my Creator knew me. I was on both the teachers and artist's path, and so, I was being provided with learning experiences in the spiritual realm... "art supplies" that might provide inspiration to others through my teaching and creative endeavors.

3. Can you recall a moment when you successfully moved out of your "victim" posture and into one of trust and gratitude? What did it feel like? What was the outcome?

4. Describe a time that you received just the right gift at just the right time.

5. At the next time you find yourself in "victim," try using the memory of your "right gift at the right time experience" to shift yourself into gratitude. Record your results.

The next two tales also have a touch of the holiday spirit.

How Great Thou Art

I was enjoying increased recognition for my paintings and fiber art. My career took me to far-flung shows in Philadelphia, New York and the DC area as well as to closer ones in southwest Virginia.

But I still didn't feel quite comfortable in gallery settings. I felt shy and unknowledgeable about the technical aspects of handling and hanging a show. And I felt intimidated by curators and gallery managers.

One day, I decided this had to change. I had a passing thought that it might be good to have some experience with managing a gallery myself. I turned it over and didn't give it another thought until two days later when I got a phone call.

It was the area's Art Gallery Queen, the Coordinator of a yearly regional art exhibit. She was going to Texas for the winter. Would I take over this year?

I would, and I did.

All manner of good things came out of this experience, including lots of fun and camaraderie with the artists of the Roanoke and New River Valleys, The New River Arts Council, and the two partners I invited to work with me.

In addition, a feature writer for the Roanoke Times/ New River Current showed up at the exhibit, loved my stuff and wrote a full-color multiple page cover story on my work.

This gratitude stuff was really working, and I was paying attention with amusement and delight as everyday miracles continued to occur.

The Love Guru

On a December afternoon one year, I surveyed the snow-covered forest outside my picture window and thought, *it's a big world out there. I'd like to live right here in the mountains...and make my living by writing books. I'd like to travel to faraway places and meet interesting people and in between my travels, come home to my cozy nest.*

I reflected that though I knew I was a good teacher, public speaker, and writer, I had a tendency to put "successful authors" on a pedestal, as though they were a different species. I thought it might be good for me to have some opportunities to break down this imaginary boundary. Perhaps if I could rub elbows with someone who had already achieved recognition, hang out a little, have a little conversation, I'd get over this, and allow myself to work toward my goal of reaching a wider audience. Once again, I sent this thought out, turned it over, and forgot it.

Within a week or two of this my husband, son and I were in New York City at my sister Kitsy's. My brother-in-law Norris had a question about Christmas Eve. Would it be OK if we spent a quiet Christmas Eve with Harville Hendrix, his wife, Helen Hunt and their kids? Harville and Norris were friends and had worked together on a video project about Harville's work.

Would it? I was reading Harville's brilliant book on marriage, **Finding the Love You Want**. It was my current favorite book. I loved it! In it, I found so much food for thought I'd pause every few pages to savor and integrate the material.

I had noticed many parallels between Imago therapy and a peer counseling technique, which was the format of the classes I was teaching at that time. So, we had some points of common interest and conversation as we hung out drinking Mystic Sodas, while our kids played together. I found him a sweet and sincere man, and I liked Helen too. She was smart, beautiful, kind...and playful.

As were collecting our coats Helen twirled around a few times in my wearable art cape, capping off the totally delightful evening...an evening in which had I had more than accomplished my goal.

Authors, even famous ones, even my very favorite ones, the ones I most respected...were people. And since they were like me, and I was like them, perhaps I was one of them, after all. I could believe it now.

6. Describe a boundary that you have dissolved, allowing you to move forward.

7. Describe, or imagine a moment when an admired icon became a "regular person" for you (in a good way!). What shifts did you notice within yourself?

Eagle Eyes

Omega Institute is the world's foremost educational retreat center, located on 195 acres of exquisite beauty in New York's Hudson Valley. I had my eyes set on this prestigious setting for a solo art exhibit. I knew that Omega's guests and distinguished presenters would appreciate my work. Like a mother who wants to honor and support her children, I wanted this for my creative babies.

I called Amina Eagle, the curator of Omega's art exhibits and proposed a show. I wanted to show her the actual pieces, as they are so lively that slides and photos can barely contain them.

She was like the fabled yogic master on the mountaintop who tries to dissuade the would-be student. She did her best to discourage me.

"It's a long way from Virginia to Rhinebeck."

"I'm willing to make the trip."

"We are deluged with applicants. There's little chance your work will be selected."

"I'm willing to take that risk."

"Don't expect to make money,"

"I just want your people to see my work."

"It'll just be me viewing the pieces. You'd have to come all the way back again to hang the show in the summer."

"That OK, I'm willing to do that."

"It's wintertime. We're in the mountains. There could be snow."

"I live in the mountains. I'm used to snow. I'm willing to drive through a blizzard, if necessary."

"OK" she said. "Come on up."

A few weeks and a ten hour drive later, I pulled my white Subaru 4 wheel drive into the white-covered parking lot on Omega's campus. I schlepped my paintings up the stairs in the administration building and spread them out for Amina to see. She looked without comment for about ten minutes. Then, I offered her my resume and clippings. She waved them away.

"I don't need to see any of that," she said. "I made up my mind right away. Your work speaks for itself, and it belongs here. And, I'd like you to come and stay for a month as Artist-in-Residence. In addition to your show, you'll be teaching staff development classes. Would you be interested?"

It was the first of two stints I did at Omega, displaying my work and teaching my own curriculum: Visionary Art and Practical Sacred Space. That year, the month of May was magic. I fell in love with my students and they fell in love with me.

When I went to leave, I couldn't find Amina. I left campus and went over the bridge...and pulled into a parking lot outside a big box store in Kingston, feeling that something was missing. I wanted to thank Amina.

Should I go in, buy a card and send it on en route? Should I go back on campus and try to find her again? And then, I realized that her car was right alongside mine and she was in it. We both got out and hugged each other. I was so happy to see her!

"I want to thank you, Amina. This experience was life-changing. This was the first time that I really felt **community**."

"Thank you," she said. "You showed up. That's what it takes for community. Showing up." It was a beautiful moment.

8. Recall a moment when your desire and confidence were so strong that you initiated something new, even though others may have tried to dissuade you.

9. Describe a time when someone whose opinion you respected recognized your talents and abilities.

10. Write about a positive experience you had in community or one you'd like to have.

11. List 5 things that you are willing to do to support your goals.

Bye-Bye, Baba

"You are never alone or helpless. The force that guides the stars, guides you, too."
P.R. Sarkar

One autumn afternoon in 1990, I was doing my meditation and something unexpected happened. I experienced a wave of Big Love. It had a specific character which I can best describe as paternal approval. I recognized the loving presence. It too, had a specific character. It was my spiritual teacher, Baba.

It had been many years since I had even thought of him. As you may remember, I was never much of a guru person. I found the organization increasingly cult-like, and over the several years of my participation, my involvement became more and more peripheral.

Unlike many of my friends and fellow yogis, I never went to India, and I never met the man, though he did show up several times as a dream guide.

Shamanlike, his appearance would change from dream to dream, but always there was no mistaking him. His dream "costumes" could not disguise his identity, and that was not their purpose. The characters and costumes he assumed served to illustrate and underscore the lesson within the dream.

His personae always carried messages that encouraged my discernment, ability to think for myself, empowerment and the healthy individuation. Never did they support the guru worship I saw going on. Nor did they condone blind rule-following.

My Baba seemed quite different from the Baba who founded and presided over the organization. I didn't know quite what to make of this, but I knew I had to do what was right for me. I decided to part ways with the yoga society.

I resigned myself to thinking that the "real" head of this organization was human, had history, grew up in a particular culture and despite his obvious spiritual advancement, had some ego, all of which influenced his decisions and organizational style.

My inner Baba seemed to be a separate entity, an inner archetype. Perhaps it was his Higher Self? Was it the part of him that was above ego, culture, and divisions? These questions would probably never be answered, and that would have to be OK.

When I left the organization, it was with no rancor. I took what I liked, the meditation and the parts of the philosophy that made sense to me, and left the rest. Mentally and formally, I said "Thank you and goodbye." And from that moment on I had no more Baba dreams, at least not ones that I remember.

So here I was, feeling his presence after all these years. Not dreaming, but quite awake. And for the first time in my waking consciousness, I felt this *intense* feeling of parental approval for me and my work…in all its irreverence, its commitment to empowerment, and its appreciation of worldly life.

"Keep going," was the thought message. "You're on the right track. I love you and I love what you're doing."

I didn't know what to make of it. But I felt happy and I allowed myself to take it in and make it mine. Three days later, I got a call from a friend, who had also been a member of the yoga society, informing me of Baba's passing.

"I thought you might want to know that Baba died three days ago," he said.

So, there was my answer. There was a connection between the man and the dream teacher.

I'm sure he visited many, many people that day. I felt happy and grateful to have been one of them. Self-approval had already taken up residence within me. I did not need to have it officially sanctioned. And yet, it was nice to have it recognized as an important principle by someone I had grown to love and respect and to know that he loved and respected me, too.

> 12. Have you ever felt the loving presence of someone who has passed? If so, describe your experience. If not, invent an experience like this you might enjoy.

House for Sale!

One challenge to abundance consciousness is the belief that if it doesn't work at our first attempt, that we should give up. If at first you don't succeed, try it again...in a different way.

My husband and I were ready to make a location change to support our creative projects at the same time our son was also ready to fly the nest. The job situation in our new location lined up right away. We made an appointment with a realtor. She gave us a very lowball estimate. It wasn't going to be enough to make it work.

I knew the right way would open, and I taking actions to facilitate our move. I drove our excess stuff up to the top of our long gravel driveway and had a yard sale to lighten our load.

One of the shoppers, Eddie, lingered and chatted with me. I told him about the underestimate of our property's worth by the realtor.

"You just have the wrong realtor," Eddie said. "You need someone who understands the value of country beauty. I know your property. It's special."

Eddie game me the name of a different realtor. David arrived, got out of his truck and looked around. I could see him out the window getting the feel of the place.

The moment he sat down with us, I knew he was the right person. He advertised our property in the paper as "Thoreau's Dream," which it truly was. And he got us a deal at our full asking price in three days.

13. Describe a time when you held out for what you really wanted.

14. Write about an experience of meeting a "right person" who brought goodness into your life.

15. Appreciate your home. What's wonderful about it? If you wanted to sell it, what would you say about it? If you don't own a home, describe something else that you value, love and appreciate.

Instant Manifestation & the Spiritual Accountant

A few years later, I had established a regional practice, with multiple offices in the Catskills. As in Virginia, everywhere I drove was beautiful. One evening, I was on my way home from my Poughkeepsie office, driving up the east bank of the Hudson River, to our place near Woodstock.

As I watched the sunset in a reverie of beauty and contentment as I drove, musing that it would be nice to have an accountant that gets me and what I do. A spiritual guy.

When I arrived at home, there was a message from an accountant's wife. She wanted to do weight loss sessions with me. They are close friends to this day… and of course, he is my "spiritual accountant."

16. Write about an accountant, hairdresser, massage therapist, other professional person in your life whom you really appreciate.

Roses for Mother

One of the most common challenges to creating abundance is the erroneous belief that we are alone and that we must tackle all our obstacles without help. We all have spirit guides, angels and archetypal energies who work with us when we ask for and are willing to receive their help.

Simply to become aware of this can be an abundance trigger. And as we share stories and experiences of these interactions, we can more easily build our confidence, trust and enthusiasm.

This story and the next few stories demonstrate how loved we are and how this love can show up as inspiration, protection, guidance, encouragement, and mentoring, both spiritual and professional.

One day I was going to meet a client I'll call Beth for a session in my office. I had a very strong sense that the Divine Mother wanted to work with Beth and that her energy would benefit the session.

In her honor, and to let her know I welcomed her help, I dabbed a tiny droplet of rose oil on my wrist. It was a very small amount, practically a homeopathic dose. Only the faintest of fragrance was discernable, when I put my nose directly to my wrist. I wanted the oil more as a symbol than as a scent.

About halfway through the Guided Meditation, an intense scent of roses filled the room, along with palpable aura of peace and love. When Beth opened her eyes they were filled with joy. I wondered whether my experience had been purely subjective or whether Beth had felt it too.

"What was that like for you?" I asked. Did you notice anything unusual?

"Roses," she said. "That was extraordinary! The Divine Mother came to visit!"

Buckle Up!

I work with angels. I don't always see them, but I can feel them and hear them. When I do see them they do not appear to me as winged beings, but as orbs of light. I always ask them to help in sessions with clients.

Whether I do this silently or in spoken word depends on the client. I ask in the interview if the client has a sense of the presence of loving celestial energy and I use his or her response as my guideline.

You may be interested to know that most people I've asked tell me that they do have a sense of the presence of angels. They express a strong desire for angelic assistance with whatever we are working on. Some of my clients see them in the same orb-like form that I do.

In the interview process, I asked a client I'll call Kitty my standard "OK to invoke angels?" question. Kitty, an attractive woman, was dressed appropriately for work. Her ash blond hair was back in an elegant French twist. She looked like she sprang from the pages of a Talbot's catalogue: neat, feminine, and upscale preppy.

"Of course, I'm comfortable with angels, "she said. "An angel saved my life. Would you like to hear what happened?"

I put down my notepad and pen, and leaned forward.

"I was driving my SUV on a country road. I hit some ice. I went into a really bad skid. The car spun around several times. When I went into the skid I was not wearing a seat belt. When I came out of it my belt was fastened."

> 17. Have you ever felt protected? If yes, describe your story. If not, describe a favorite myth, fairy tale or spiritual story about Divine protection.

The Mysterious Moving CDs

This story illustrates the connection between forgiveness and abundance and that our guidance will do what it takes to get us to pay attention...even if that means making us laugh!

I continued to explore New Thought principles and apply them. One morning, I asked my inner guidance to teach me more about prosperity consciousness. What could I play with? What could I apply in the learning laboratory called "my life"? Later that day, my then husband Murray and I went out to dinner and a movie in nearby Christiansburg, Virginia.

When we arrived at home, we saw something unusual on the floor of the living room, in front of the CD rack. Fanned out in a crescent shape, like a deck of cards, was an array of CDs! The music CDs were all in place on the rack. Only the spiritual CDs from the bottom section of the rack were in this "spread."

Curious! We had no pets. Our son was grown and out of the house. No one other than Murray and I had the key. Nothing else had been moved. The configuration of the CDs was orderly and perfectly formed.

I had the impression that I was to choose the one that best answered my question. I ran my hands over the CDs and felt their energy. I knew which one to choose when my hand hovered over "Deep Profound Forgiveness" by Edwene Gaines and I got a happy "yes!" sensation followed by a feeling of peace.

I picked up the CD and asked Murray if he minded if I put the Guided Imagery on while we relaxed before sleep. He agreed. Before I left the living room, I replaced the CDs and tucked them well back in their places, putting a Reiki music CD on top of the spiritual section.

As I drifted off to sleep, listening to the gentle imagery, I felt a lovely shift in my heart center. In the morning, I padded through the living room on my way to make my morning coffee. And there, I saw another surprise!

All the CDs were still in their places but one. The top CD was pulled forward, in "Pick Me!" position. Only it wasn't the Reiki CD. It was my guides' **symbolic shorthand** for this lesson: Forgiveness is an essential component in the prosperity process. It was a prosperity CD by Edwene Gaines!

I never before or since had CDs from this rack shift positions, fall on the floor or otherwise move in any way. It was only this one time. I got the message and it has served me well.

18. Describe an experience when forgiving someone brought goodness into your life in some way.

Dream Girl

Do you ever feel like you have to figure everything out? Worry about making the right decisions in your work? Here's a story about the infinite help and guidance available and ready to help you.

I had a client, Shirley, who had great success working with me. She had a deep understanding of New Thought Principles and responded extremely well to Guided Imagery and Energy Work.

One day, she called me to set up some sessions for her teenage daughter, Diane. The girl wanted to do some work related to owning her inner beauty.

This is a program I've done for years, and even presented workshops on, so I was certainly ready with material in a general sense. As always, though, I wanted to personalize her session and grow beyond anything I'd done before in terms of imagery.

I had a slight case of butterflies about the session. Shirley was such a great client. But who knew how it would go with Diane? Did Shirley have expectations? Was Diane even really interested? This was so not like me! I realized that my ego was involved and resolved to clear it out of the equation.

The night before the session, I did my prep work for the session right before bedtime. When I said my prayers, I asked for help with Diane. Specifically, I wanted to feel a sense of rapport with her, so that my intuition would be in synch with hers. I also asked for inspiration for appropriate imagery for her. Perhaps there an angel who might be of particular help?

In my dream, I saw Hannah, a close friend from first grade all the way through high school. The dream began in black and white. It opened with the yearbook photo of Hannah standing outside the school wearing a dark pea jacket. Then the photos came to life. Hannah's long, shiny brown hair began blowing in a gentle breeze.

She turned to look at me and smiled, as she changed into a full-color image, hair now glinting with natural chestnut highlights. She was a dreamgirl; the epitome of beauty, an eighteen year-old goddess.

And now...the mind movie zoomed in to a close face shot of Hannah. Only her face was changing! The dreamgirl still had shiny, beautiful hair. But her face changed into that of another teenage girl, a few years younger, one whom I'd never before met.

She was looking at me, face to face, eyes to eyes, very close up. We looked at each other for what seemed like a very long time, taking each other in, connecting. Then, I woke up.

While I ate my breakfast, I looked at an angel book, thinking maybe I'd find something I could use in some guidance about which angel to call into the session. There, I found an entry on the angel of Beauty: Haniel. Apparently Haniel was already on the job as her symbolic representative had already visited me!

Hannah, I mused, had always been beautiful, even as a small child. Her house was beautiful, her parents were beautiful and so were her siblings.

In her teens, and early twenties, she blossomed into a talented artist and lovely young woman. So, it made sense that my intuitive self had chosen her image as iconic shorthand for "youthful feminine beauty."

When I arrived at my office building and began walking up the stairs, I could hear Shirley's voice and those of a man and a young girl.

Diane and her parents had arrived and awaited me. At the top of the stairs, there she was: the girl in my dreams! The one who showed me her face, her energy, and her soul.

My prayers had been answered. I had received all that I asked for, and more: inspired imagery, angelic assistance and rapport, and a pre-meeting meeting! She loved working with me, and the feeling was mutual. We did good work, and I was grateful.

19. Can you remember a time when you met someone for the first time and felt a sense of rightness and familiarity? Write about this.

Showtime Times Two!
One: The Ringing Phone

Part of prosperity consciousness is recognizing that our flow of good is there for us, even if we don't see it at the moment. Learning to trust that all is well.

Several years ago, I was working on a series of paintings for an art show. I was in a happy flow, enjoying the process and loving the work that was emerging, a vibrant series of portraits. I'd already counted how many canvasses it would take for a great-looking exhibit and I wasn't quite sure how I'd do it by Showtime.

Due to an unusually open schedule, I was on track for my deadline. Several days went by without a client booking. I got a little nervous for a moment...and then decided to trust.

I turned my scheduling over to God, gave thanks for the time, and painted with gusto. Just as I was finishing up the last painting, the phone began to ring off the hook with clients wanting sessions!

The rest of the story? The show went well. And there was a surprise visitor: the Governor of Virginia, Mark Warner, who did a one-on-one walkthrough of the paintings with me, talking about the pieces and admiring on my work!

Two: Mission Possible

Last fall, a logistical need arose to store a large number of paintings for five months. A storage locker was out of the question. I needed to place them in a safe, climate controlled area, where someone could keep an eye on them. Better yet, I thought, a lot of someones, and lots of eyes, who would enjoy looking at them.

What if I could find a place for an exhibit? It was the middle of September. My window would begin in November and end in late March. Most art shows are planned many months, sometimes *years*...in advance. And most exhibits last a month or two at the most. Impossible situation?

I contacted the curator of the gallery space at a University Library and the proprietor of the coolest restaurant in town. Would they host shows of my art for the duration? And both of these awesome men said yes. Just like that, done.

California Paradise & the Venus Effect

When it comes to manifestation, the magic stance is like that of a tennis champ. Alert, loose, open to respond to what *is*, not what s/he expects or demands. Tennis pros don't refuse to return the ball (or fail to recognize its existence!) unless it appears conveniently on their dominant side.

They're ready for the backhand or to race to the net, if that's what's called for. Anything can happen and that's what makes the game interesting and fun. Nor should we affix attachment to any one of the infinite possibilities that are there for us. Joyous anticipation of the good that awaits us *in whatever form* it may appear is a wonderful abundance trigger!

We cannot know all the possibilities available and that's OK. It's our job to ask for what we want, or something even better that we may not have considered even remotely possible!

A client I'll call Liz was relocating to the LA area. Her work had moved her to temporary digs for a limited time. We discussed her preferences: attractive, close to work, affordable, preferably furnished, in a place where she could meet copacetic, open-minded people and become part of the local holistic community. She wanted connection and privacy, in a place where she could nurture herself, grow spiritually, and enjoy life.

Normally an upbeat, rather easygoing woman, she'd been looking in her time off work and was feeling tired and pressed for time. In two weeks she'd either need to find a place or commit to staying where she was for longer than she wanted to. I inferred from her readiness to be done with this that she was, in fact, about to find her perfect nest. And so, she was.

Urgency is an interesting emotion. You can choose to feel it, ego style, as a passive victim, beset by fate unknown and dreaded. Or you can opt for a sense of glorious adventure. Liz, who is becoming quite the spiritual "tennis player," chose this stance. We anchored it together and turned it over.

That weekend, she struck California Gold. For **three hundred dollars a month less** than the going rate for a so-so studio, she snagged a nicely appointed private space in a huge house owned by a man of kindness and integrity.

The house is only twelve minutes from Liz's place of work. It comes with the use of a swimming pool and waterfall, storage space, common kitchen, dining and entertainment areas (big screen TV and giant DVD collection) interesting, congenial roommates, and (are you ready for this?) ***food***!

Gourmet, restaurant quality food, as it turns out. The homeowner (who is also a roommate and now, a friend) fills the fridge with fresh, delicious fare and is happy to make special request purchases. Whoever feels like cooking, cooks. Most meals are prepared by a roommate who just happens to be a professional chef! Liz is very happy in her new home.

Your Abundance Stories

Recall and write about some abundance stories in your life. Illustrate your favorites stories, if you feel so moved.

20. A time when a door opened for you...

21. When you lost something and something even better flowed into place...

22. A happy synchronicity...

Abundance Triggers

23. An answered prayer...

24. The discovery of a hidden talent...

25. An unexpected success...

26. A time you felt happy about an accomplishment you worked hard for...

27. A time you succeeded at something with great ease...

28. An experience that surprised and delighted you...

29. An aha!...

30. A time when you found just what you wanted for just the right price.

31. A gift you received...

32. A gift you gave...

33. An uplifting experience...

34. A warm and loving experience...

35. Something about your life that makes you feel rich...

36. Something about your life that makes you feel blessed...

37. Something about your life that makes you feel loved...

Add stories to your journal anytime they occur. You can include your own demonstrations, those of friends and those you hear or read about. You'll find them in myths, fairy tales, and in spiritual books. Collecting and remembering abundance stories is, in itself, an abundance trigger.

Chapter 4

Desire and Deservingness

"Desire is the starting point of all achievement, not a hope, not a wish, but a keen pulsating desire which transcends everything."

- Napoleon Hill

To accomplish anything, we must desire. Desire is the creative impulse within. It is that energetic impulse to extend love though work and word, through creation and procreation, and through building true community.

And before we can desire, we must first acknowledge ourselves. We must be… and accept our being. It is within the warm womb of self-acceptance that we prepare to give birth to new life, as who we are to be in the world.

We are born into a world of duality, which likes to divide and compare, presenting us with experiences of contrast. As we bump up against what we don't want, we discover more about the personalities we ride in. What we like, what we don't like, what we feel moved to do. This is precious information. In it are clues for the treasure hunt of self-discovery.

Your Unique Fabulosity & the Three Levels of Mind

The mental mind likes to count, categorize, divide and separate. He's a man; she's a woman. This is a flower; that's a rock. My ancestry is Pennsylvania German, Welsh and English. Yours is what it is. The heart can appreciate that you and I are amazing. It knows that there is beauty in you and beauty in me, regardless of our ancestral origins and other details. It can love. The spiritual mind knows only Oneness. It IS Love, formless, eternal and changeless.

So, here we are (or seem to be), infinite expressions of the One, beautiful in our rich diversity. We are learning recognize the light that shines through each of us, to respect our unique fabulosity and that of every one of our brothers and sisters, and to find our way home.

Entitlement

"You are the light of the world."
-Jesus

Entitlement has a bad rap. Your ego isn't entitled, but your real self is. You come from spirit. You are spirit. You are the son or daughter of God. You are entitled to abundance of ***every*** kind, including spiritual bliss. Yes, you are. That's true entitlement. That's your birthright.

The ego's false entitlement says to the "other," "I'm special," meaning "I'm more special than others. "I'm God, and you're not. I'm THE God, so do as I say or you'll be sorry!" It wants only to take. It's empty. Because It doesn't know that it's in the womb of God, it believes itself to be in terrible danger, all alone and struggling for its very survival.

So even though it only takes, it has nothing. It has nothing because it cannot access the wealth within… without a shift of consciousness.

Your House is a Very, Very, Very Fine House

If you inherited a beautiful piece of property would you let the house crumble for lack of care? Would you let weeds grow up and take over? Would you let it sit vacant, while you lived in a hole in the ground? Of course not!

You are the homeowner. You are always home, wherever you go. You have inherited a fortune and there is a mansion awaiting you. The key is self-acceptance.

Les Miserables

(The ego's) old paradigm consumer culture is set up to contradict this. Turn on the television to almost any show or commercial. What is being sold is need, "not enoughness," anger, jealousy, fear, shame and products to feed and perpetuate these emotions.

And oh, does it like drama! The drama of politics, war and suffering get played out on TV and in our minds as long as we stay stuck in ego. To live in abundance consciousness, you have to change the channel. Why would anyone watch the Misery show, anyway?

It's sort of like cigarettes. You have to shut off your senses of taste and smell to keep smoking. Once you reawaken and really notice how foul it is, continuing to smoke becomes an unacceptable option. Choosing to become an abundant thinker is like choosing to become a Fresh Air Breather.

So, since the false ego is the enemy of abundance, let's tune up our sensibilities, declare its true nature as toxic smoke of the deluded mind, turn on the fan and open the windows. It's a nice day out there. You might want to go out and play!

The False Ego as Drama Junkie: One Step Over the Borderline

The essential abandonment wound is self-inflicted by the false ego. So, the wound is illusory. You can wake up into a happier dream.

The false ego loves suffering and seeks to fuel it. You might say it has a personality disorder. It has imagined itself to be set apart from Source, so it believes itself to be separate, without identity of its own, doomed to be forever separated from Love.

Talk about a feeling of falling out of the universe! And, so, it experiences separation anxiety on a cosmic level. Like a lost child, it fears for its very survival.

And like a child, it is ultrasensitive to stimuli. Delays feel like denials. Everything is taken personally. Molehills become mountains. Thinking is black or white. People are good or bad.

For the ego, normal boundaries are perceived as rejection and abandonment. It is entirely unaware that the "abandonment" is imagined and projected; projection is what it does.

It projects its fear on the world and the "other." It projects its rage on the "other" and imagines God to be harsh and punishing. It expects punishment from this mean God and takes on the job itself. The self-imposed agony of aloneness and lack of trust in self, God and "other" wreak havoc in every area of life.

It doesn't believe itself worthy of love and yet cannot stand the agony of its imagined separation. And so it seduces, charms, commandeers, takes "love" hostages and sooner or later drives them away, further justifying its victim posture, belief in being unfairly treated and its desire for revenge. Whether it identifies as "Victim/Rescuer/Fixer" (codependent) or "Justified Punisher" (abuser) doesn't matter. It's the same ego in different dress.

Compassion for the Scared/Sacred Child.

And however it may disguise itself, it comes down to a basic error. A mistake, made by a childlike ego. A child who wants its parent and isn't sure how to get home, or that it would be welcomed if it could find its way.

As with a raging child who hits and bites, it must be interrupted and prevented from continuing its attempts to harm. And it must receive what it so desperately needs: boundaries, empathy, compassion and reeducation as to its actual safety.

This dynamic works on the personal, national and global levels. "Justified Punishers" abound and it's all too easy to spot the projections, distortion campaigns and vilification the Perpetrator part of our collective ego so enjoys.

Most of all, the ego is a like prodigal child who believe s/he deserves to be locked out. When s/he is not projecting on others, s/he self-punishes. S/he thinks s/he is unworthy. S/he will make up stories about why s/he is unworthy and create "justified self-punishments." The stories are all a variation of "there's something wrong with me."

For example, the belief that "I'm ugly" can show up for women as "I'm too fat, too flat-chested or too skinny" or for men as too short, too weak, too "average." And of course, "I'm not enough" can show up as "I don't have enough."

Authentic entitlement says, *"I'm plenty, and I'm connected to the vast universal plenty."* And so, there is plenty.

Shame & Success:
"Who Do You Think You Are?" Syndrome

It's possible to concentrate one's attention in short spurts and attract goodies for a while. For lasting happiness, though, it takes an upleveling of consciousness.

I have noticed in myself and others that successes are sometimes followed by a let-down. When one succeeds beyond previous self-imposed boundaries, it's important check for unconscious limiting beliefs and to make necessary adjustments, to allow for ownership and enjoyment of success and to pave the way for more successes.

Some of these beliefs may be:

"I don't deserve this."

"I am acting outside my designated role in life. I'm not allowed to be this successful and I will be punished for it."

"I'm out of my league. Successful people are different. Time to retreat."

You do deserve it. If you are a woman and your role in the family was Cinderella, go to the ball. Don't retreat; refresh. Put on a little lipstick maybe, get in that nice orange carriage and have yourself some fun! Men, please translate this into terms that work for you.

A.R.E. You Experienced?

One way to heal "Who Do You Think You Are?" Syndrome is to ask yourself that question replacing the contemptuous tone with one of actual self-appreciating curiosity. Deep inside, you know how wonderful you are.

Properly asked, the question becomes an invitation to be your best you, your real you. This story illustrates the prospering power of reclaiming WDYTYA? And using it as rocket fuel.

Many years ago, I had a show at the Heritage Center in Virginia Beach. I enjoyed the experience and was especially happy that the owner/founder of the Heritage Store and Center, Tom Johnson became a collector. And what followed took me to a whole new level of happy.

I got a call from the curator of art exhibits at the Association for Research and Enlightenment. She loved my work. Would I consider doing a solo show there?

My excitement stirred up an even stronger desire.

"I'd love to, and I'd love to do more. I'd like to do some workshops at the A.R.E. about shifting into abundance consciousness using creativity."

"That would really fit with the manifestation theme of our New Years' Conference. We're calling it "Expect a Miracle."

I made a proposal and it was accepted. I was to do two workshops. "Creating Sacred Space for Manifestation" on Saturday afternoon and "Treasure Mapping" on Sunday.

I got comfortable with the conference hall when I went to hang the art show in November. I'd been doing workshops for a long time by now, some of which were in pretty big venues. It was a logical step and one I was ready to take.

My contact person told me to expect a smallish enrollment of about 25, because it was New Year's and there's so much going on at that time of the year. Then, I got a call that there were 49 sign-ups for my workshops. "Are you game?" she said.

"Sure, no problem. The more, the merrier."

I guess someone was listening.

A few weeks passed and I got another call.

"We have 250 people signed up now. That's capacity. Are you OK with that?"

"Absolutely!"

And I was. It was fun. It was fun being written up in the A.R.E. magazine. It was fun to adapt my workshop so that a large number of participants could stay engaged and excited.

It was fun seeing my headshot and bio next to that of headliner Dan Millman, author of the bestselling book **The Way of the Peaceful Warrior**. It was fun to sign my contract. I was feeling frisky.

Until I got there and WDYTYA? Syndrome kicked in. Something about meeting the Masculine called up self-doubt. My was soul calling me to acknowledge that feeling and to get over it. I met Dan, robust and radiating manly can-do energy as we shook hands. Enough energy to power Brooklyn.

On Friday, I went to Mark Thurston's presentation. His Masculine was equally impressive. Uber-intelligent, carefully organized and articulate. The man could probably do the **New York Times** crossword with a pen.

That night, I skipped Dan's workshop in favor of preparation of my own. I went back to my room, looked at my notes and despaired. *What was I thinking, coming here? Who do I think I am on a program with these guys?* And that's what snapped me out of it.

I realized that the A.R.E. had hired me to be me, so my best course of action would be to relax and be myself. I had something they wanted. Then, I asked myself what is that something?

"Who *do* I think I am? What is the teaching that's coming through me?" My ego took a back seat, while my Higher Self began answering these questions.

And, of course, once my stance shifted from nervous to service, I focused on my message. I took it out of its high-heeled pumps and put it in comfortable shoes. I decided it would be quite all right to be earthy, feminine, and maybe just a little bit silly.

I took my neatly printed notes, boiled them down to their barest essence and handwrote them on the yellow legal pad I use in sessions.

The next day, I barely glanced at them and then dropped them like Dumbo's feather. I flew on love and the sheer joy of sharing. It was magic. Afterwards, two A.R.E. veterans told me that in twenty-eight years of workshops they had never seen, heard or experienced a better speaker.

1. Describe a time when your decision to be yourself resulted in a good outcome.

2. Name three qualities that identify your You-ness. Honor and appreciate them.

3. Recall a time when you realized a "magical" power you mistakenly ascribed to an outside crutch was really within you...and you let go. Or, describe an experience like this that you would like to have.

Letting Go of Limiting Beliefs

"If the doors of perception were cleansed, everything would appear to man as it is, infinite."
    -William Blake

It's All Good:
The "Detour" and the Tour!

A common limiting belief is that we get to make the plan and control how it comes. This stance says: there are good things on our plan, and bad things, not on our plan. Straight shot, good; detours, bad.

The truth is, we do get to state our preferences and consciously create goals. We don't get to control the method by which our good arrives.

Sometimes goals get met quickly and directly, as in some of the stories I shared with you. Sometimes, our prayers are answered with experiences that call us to uplevel our awareness and to learn new skills, as I shared in my book, **Surviving Cancer and Other Tough Stuff**.

The ego loves to pose as an unfairly treated victim, not only of people but of circumstances...a victim of life itself. It misses the point of detours. Detours are a vital part of the tour! They are gifts of the soul, responses to prayer, calls to Becoming.

They provide us unimaginable richness. They give us opportunities to connect with important allies, friends and loved ones. They help us to learn. In these detours, we acquire crucial tools for life that we can practically apply in the achievement of our goals.

4. Recount a life "detour" in which you learned something valuable, met someone wonderful or just plain had fun!

Keepin' it Real: Acknowledging "Negative" Feelings

Another limiting belief is that negative feelings are "bad," and that we're not supposed to have them, if we want to be prosperous. The truth is that burying these feelings creates problems. It's another way of hanging onto them and inadvertently giving them power.

Perhaps the most challenging of all "negative" emotions is anger. When we are early in our spiritual growth learning curve, we may hold onto resentments and painful relationships so we can fully milk our martyrdom. We may attach to an angry person and let him or her act out on us, so it can be "the other" who holds the rage we refuse to own.

Or, we may cherish anger, even to the point of making it our religion and homeland, rolled into one…carrying a banner of "justified rage" as we ride into a seemingly endless series of needless battles, finding fault wherever we go.

I'm sure that readers of this book are well aware that vitriol poisons the well of abundance. And I'm guessing that if you're interested in prosperous thinking, you're most likely making a genuine effort to practice kindness and compassion.

While In terms of the outer world, taking the high road is generally the best choice, the inner path to abundance does not bypass or deny natural human emotions. We are, as Jacquelyn Small observed, "spiritual beings having a human experience." And so, we must come to terms with our humanness as well as our spirituality.

"Spiritual Bypass" & Faux Forgiveness

Small also coined the term, "spiritual bypass." When we attempt to ignore our "negative" emotions and skip over them instead of working through them, we end up with a stockpile of resentment we're not aware of that will block the flow of our good if we don't take responsibility to own it and clear it.

Our culture celebrates irresponsible anger. Just as television sells shame and not-enoughness, so it also sells anger.

Turn on the television on any given day and you can see models of rage and resentment, blame and shame, gossip and gall. Where are the models of healthy anger? The kind that gives us the energy required to set boundaries, request change, and when necessary, move ourselves out of disharmonious situations, and create new and better ones?

Getting Your "Happy" Back

One afternoon, while flipping channels between CMT and VH1 as I worked out to videos, I came upon a compelling empowerment anthem. Carrie Underwood, spectacular in a silver mini-dress, belted out her platinum hit **"Undo it,"** the song of a woman well on the way to reclaiming her "happy" after a bad relationship.

Underwood, who was in her college days a Magna Cum Laude Mass Communication major with an emphasis in journalism, certainly knows how to tell a story in a way that really connects with an audience.

Her song eloquently expresses the energy surge that we call "anger" being utilized purposefully, in the service of making positive changes and moving on.

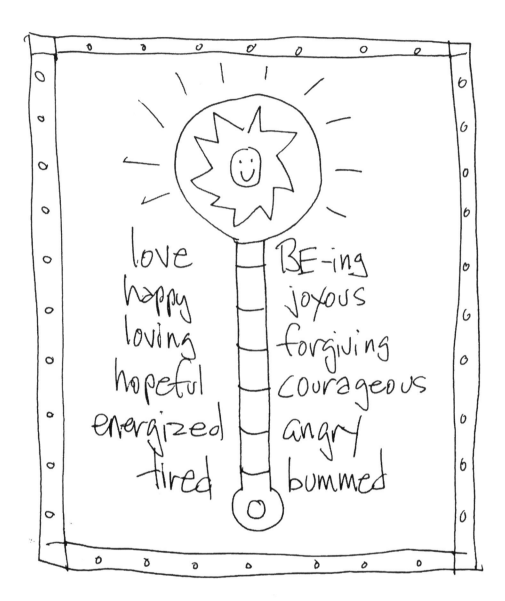

Up the Feeling Scale

It's all about movement, and it's important not to hang out in the anger zone too long. Anyone who's familiar with the principle that like attracts like understands that anger junkies attract more "reasons" to be angry!

Move through it and beyond it, keep on going up the feeling scale and before you know it, you will be an irresistible abundance magnet.

Using the country music metaphor, a woman (or man) betrayed may begin her healing process in numbness. She may move up the scale to sadness. Further up, she may feel rage and even harbor revenge fantasies *("Before He Cheats")*.

"I Hope you Dance"...

As she continues to accept her feelings they keep moving up the scale...to healthy anger, courage, hope, renewal, vitality, happiness and joy. Love for her now is generalized to all of humanity.

She may have a "special relationship" with a mate...and even so, her loves extends to everyone. She dances, and it is her hope that you dance, too. *From this level on the scale of emotions, miracles are the rule, not the exception.*

...and Kick

Letting go of the habit of suppressing "negative" emotion is as important as letting go of the habit of acting it out, cherishing it or staying stuck in it. The first step is to let go of the limiting beliefs that it's not OK to feel anger, or that it's OK to act it out on people (others and/or yourself).

The following are some other limiting beliefs that people may have around abundance. The last two on the list (having to do with worthiness), are particularly potent.

Limiting Beliefs & Your Authentic Self

False: If I don't desire, I'll be free of suffering.

True: *You come here to engage and contribute. Desire is your both your fuel and your navigational tool. It's attachment to a specific outcome that is creates suffering. Outcome is in the God Department.*

False: It is more spiritual to deny desire.

True: *Mind creates. You are Mind. To bury your creativity is to block your purpose.*

False: I'm too damaged to succeed at anything. The best I can do is to cope.

True: *You are what you think you are and how you think you are. What the mind creates, it can un-create. Do you really want to settle for "just OK" when "happy" is on the menu?*

False: I am a victim of my emotions and thoughts. They "happen to me."

True: *You can choose your emotions and thoughts. You get better at directing them with practice, so don't worry if you slip. Just keep at it and after a while, you will be happily surprised by your sense of inner peace.*

False: I must act on my emotions.

True: *You can give consideration to where the emotion is coming from and whether it serves your well-being to act on it. If it is without compassion or joy, the correct "action" is an internal one. Follow the emotion back to the thought that generated it and the belief that generated that. That's where the work is. That's where miracles come from!*

False: Successful people have no personal life.

True: *There are those who use work to fill a spiritual void and those whose spirituality fuels their work. The former cannot love others because they cannot love themselves. The latter usually have wonderful connections with others. Because they express love, they attract it. You can choose to be one of them.*

False: If I am successful, people will be jealous and I couldn't stand that. I need everyone to like me.

True: *There is a recovery saying: "What other people think of you is none of your business." If you are tiptoeing around jealous and controlling people, they already don't like you. This sort of person doesn't like anyone. Like yourself, and you will attract people who like themselves, too. They're much more fun and they will celebrate your successes!*

False: Rich people are selfish and "bad."

True: *Rich people are people with money. People are people, rich or poor. Money is convenient and fun. You might as well enjoy it!*

False: You have to choose between doing what you love and making money.

True: *Many people find ways to do both. If you really love to do something, you will put in the hours required to succeed, you will be guided as you go and doors will open for you.*

False: If I'm really spiritual, I'll just be open to whatever shows up.

True: *You are the Divine expressing as you. The highest expression of service in human life requires willingness to discover the specifics of who you are as a unique expression of Source energy and taking action on what you discover.*

False: Life is about service, not fun.

True: *Service does not mean martyrdom. Real service is an extension of real love. A measure of authenticity and wholeness is enjoyment of life. You might as well face it; when you are living as you, fun is involved.*

False: I could have, but... (some variation of I didn't have the support from the world, God or myself)

True: *Now is always the launch pad.*

False: I am separate from my Source. My flow is blocked, because I am separate from my Source. God has abandoned me.

True: *You can never be separated from your Divine Source. It is like a perpetually shining sun. Put down the umbrella, and you can enjoy it.*

Note: This last limiting belief is the one that underlies all others. Meditation is a good proactive remedy. That is the purpose for which it was designed, and it works as intended, especially when practiced for a short time each day. You'll find a basic how-to in the Resource section.

Before making your own inventory of limiting beliefs, you may find it useful to become more aware of your thoughts and patterns, with the help from your Observer.

Activating the Observer

5. Visualization: Read this once or twice to get the flow of it and then close your eyes. Take a few deep "letting go" breaths and relax your body. Let it rest while you imagine floating up into a soft white light and resting there...resting in the peace and light of Divine Love. Just be.

   When you are ready, you can gently descend, just enough to see the earth take shape, now in further, just enough to see your continent... your country...your city or county...your home...now hover above your body and see yourself resting below. See yourself in a neutral way, with love and detachment at the same time, just noticing...

   Now gently come back into your body, bringing back with you a sense of compassionate detachment. You are in your life and watching yourself live your life at the same time. You speak and you hear what you say.

   You feel and you create space around the feeling, enough for it to live and breathe, without necessarily acting on it. You can easily observe yourself in the present and you can also scan the past to notice patterns of thought and behavior.

Everything After "But" is Bull-oney!

6. Look back over the limiting beliefs True & False list to prompt your thinking. Give yourself time to reflect.

7. Write your own list of limiting beliefs in a thin-lined pen. After each entry, affirm the truth with a thicker, bolder pen.

   Here's a good one to start with:

   False: I'd like to _____, but _____.

   Truth: _____.

8. Visualization: Read this once or twice to get the gist and then gently close your eyes. Begin to breathe deeply and let your body become nicely relaxed. Imagine that you are at a bonfire, in the center of a meadow surrounded by tall trees. It's late at night and the stars create a canopy for this event. You are with a circle of friends, loved ones and mentors, your spiritual clan, who are serving as witnesses for you.

   You have prepared a releasing basket for yourself and it is on the ground at your feet. In it are three stones. Each one is wrapped in a paper. The paper is tied with string made from dried plant fibers. On each paper is written a limiting belief that you are ready to let go of.

   You pick them up one at a time, and cast them into the fire, watching the paper and string ignite and burn. The smoke goes up, like a message to the heavens. You are free now and you may move forward in the direction of your destiny. Your spiritual family sings songs of gladness and celebration for you.

From Head to Heart

Once you have the intellectual awareness that certain ideas have been limiting and you have replaced these ideas with working affirmations, it's time to make these real. For true abundance, intellectual understanding of spiritual principles needs to ground in the body.

In my early days as a yoga and meditation teacher, I sat one day in *sadhana* cross-legged on the floor on a woven mat, in my apartment on 42nd and Locust St. I faced the window, and even though my eyes were closed, the April sun poured golden warmth onto my eyelids.

I breathed in the light and breathed myself into it as I silently said my mantra. I imagined the light entering through the root chakra at the base of my spine.

As I had been taught, I moved the energy up to my second chakra…my third… at the fourth chakra, the heart center, I felt a block, pinching the energy and holding it back from fully flowing.

This uncomfortable "stuck" feeling was in my upper back. Its epicenter seemed to be located in the back half of my heart center. At that point, I realized that my ability to experience Spirit could only go so far without clearing emotional blocks.

All the philosophic study and intellectual knowledge were like a roof that needs a foundation, floor and walls to be a real house that you can live in and enjoy.

The name yoga of the society I belonged to translated from the Sanskrit as "The Path of Bliss." I wanted to walk a path of wholeness, to bring that bliss into my life and ground it. So, in that moment, I committed myself to healing and releasing as part and parcel of my spiritual practice. It was a decision that changed my life. I went head-on into the work of the heart and never stopped.

For, the place where spiritual knowledge and practice meet is in the heart. It is in the heart that Forgiveness and Self Acceptance move into Love and Gratitude. And when this happens, abundance flows.

9. Write a letter of commitment to yourself to live in abundance.

10. How does this feel in your heart?

11. What does abundance mean to you?

In the center of your heart, there lives Love and overflowing abundance. ♥

Abundance Triggers

Chapter 5

The Three Kings:

Reframing, Forgiveness & Gratitude

Reframing, Forgiveness and Gratitude are like the Three Wise Kings who travel together, bearing gifts. When the heart is opened, Reframing occurs naturally. We perceive the learnings in our experiences. Our victim stories fall away. We feel Gratitude, as we realize that our most challenging relationships have been our teachers. They helped us discover strengths, release old patterns and claim our power.

Forgiveness is the realization that there is nothing to forgive.

Forgiveness triggers abundance in many forms: money, love, career opportunities, physical vitality and wellbeing. As these next two stories illustrate, it can heal relationships between people *within* a person. When we forgive ourselves and other people, a flow of energy is released. Our hearts can contain more of the wholeness of who we are.

Follow the Breadcrumbs

Once, I had a "chance" encounter with an acquaintance in the supermarket. I was on the bread aisle, heading toward the organic milk. The night before, I'd prayed about her and made a decision to make an amends for an inadvertent mistake. I had been seen her through the eyes of another, as if this vision was the truth. As if there is an "other." As soon as I realized my error, I knew I needed to do something to make it right.

The following day, there she was, passing the bread crumbs and Wasa Crisps, within arm's reach! I said her name. She looked at me with love and kindness. She was delighted to see me and told me she'd wanted to connect as well. Apparently, both of our prayers had been answered.

"There's nothing to forgive," she said. "You couldn't have done anything to change the situation. I never blamed you."

"I guess I need to forgive myself, "I said. We both laughed.

My perception of her changed utterly in those few moments. We were good. We were sisters. On my way home, my heart center opened and began pulsing with love, bright and big. Love for her, love for the one who had lied about her, love for myself and for all humanity.

And then, I had a healing, a sort of spontaneous retrieval and integration of a soul fragment. I wrote about it in my journal.

Bunny Walks on the Wild Side

I was driving home today in soft light flurries, the pale gray sky vibrant with the promise of new life. My mind wandered as I passed by sleeping farmers' fields, suburban hamlets, and stretches of snowy woods. My hands and feet knew the way all on their own.

My peaceful heart must have invited the guest. She came to visit as I drove through deep forests. I was a bit surprised to see her after all these years.

She was dressed entirely out of season, in Villager coordinates. Navy twill skirt, navy jacket trimmed with apple green and white, navy skimmer flats with bows, fisherman's basket shoulder bag. A navy grosgrain ribbon with little white polka dots neatly secured her frosted mane. A demure and understated strand of pearls adorned her neck.

"Welcome, Bunny." I said. I call her Bunny because she's soft and sweet and fluffy. And scared stiff to be herself. Or at least she used to be. Who knows what she's been up to since the ninth grade?

It was certainly a departure, I reflected, to see her here and now. How had she fared in the country club life her father had chosen for her? What excuse had she given to slip out and visit such an artsy type as me?

She seemed excited, as if something wonderful was about to happen.

Hi, Kanta," she smiled shyly, but with a sparkle in her eyes.

"Come on in," I invited her. "Would you like to stay for tea?"

"Oh, no", she said, "I'd like to stay forever."

Then, she took her suitcase full perfect navy, apple green and pink outfits, matching grosgrain ribbons, and Papagallo flats, climbed into my heart, and made herself a cozy nest.

The woman I was groomed to be, my soul fragment, had come home.

My father, now in spirit, smiled. He too, was freed to be himself. And I thanked him for loving me so much.

1. Write the story of a time when you forgave someone and felt better.

2. Write the story of a time when you forgave yourself and felt better.

3. Visualization: Read this once or twice to get the gist and then gently close your eyes. Begin to breathe deeply and let your body become nicely relaxed.

    Bring to mind an individual against whom you have held a grudge. Imagine that your resentment becomes a liquid that is released from the cells of your body. It finds its way to the surface of your skin.

The wind and sun dry it and it becomes a fine magnetic dust on your skin's surface. Now a large magnet is lowered from above and it pulls all the resentment dust off you. The magnet returns to its skyward home.

A fresh breeze caresses your newly cleansed skin and lighter, freer body. When you're ready, come back.

4. How has your life stayed on track with parental and/or societal expectations of you?

5. How has your life differed from expectations of you?

6. Write a short "thank you letter" to yourself, appreciating your courage to be yourself.

7. Tune in empathically to someone whose expectations or behavior you that you felt uncomfortable with. What do you imagine s/he was feeling? Trying to accomplish?

   Stay with this until you can feel compassion for this person. Mentally, surround him or her with light and then release the image.

8. Write your own forgiveness visualization or exercise and use it.

9. How has someone you found challenging been a teacher to you? What did you learn?

10. Mentally thank, and then release the person.

11. Write your own soul retrieval story. Recall a time when you healed and reclaimed a "lost" part of yourself...or imagine a soul retrieval story you would like to experience.

12. Make a wholeness Mandala.

13. What are you most grateful for in your life right now?

14. Write a few sentences of appreciation for your body...

15. Your closest relationships...

16. Your mentors...

17. Your work.

18. What is your fondest dream?

19. How will you know you've achieved it?

20. Put yourself in the feeling of having achieved it.

21. Ask for Divine help, give thanks in advance, and trust.

22. Imagine some action steps you can take to achieve it.

23. Begin taking actions.

24. At each step, record what you did and appreciate yourself.

25. Continue to visualize your goal with pleasure and gratitude.

Chapter 6

Feeling & Follow-Through: Embodying Joy

"Use Your Emotional Content!"
-Bruce Lee

What does abundance feel like to you? What, when you touch it, triggers happy feelings or feelings of luxury? Satin sheets or your favorite flannel gown, fresh from the dryer? Stroking the smooth cheek of your grandchild or petting your kitty? The aroma of roast turkey or the fragrance of frankincense?

1. List eight of your favorite sense triggers for abundance.

2. Use your triggers anytime you want to put yourself into abundance consciousness.

Joyce, Joy and Jujubes

My dear friend Joyce Johnson grew up on a tobacco farm in rural North Carolina. Her mother was the founder and pastor of a church. Joyce hated tobacco and loved God.

As she matured, her God did too. He morphed from an angry old man to a loving energetic Field of Being. I met her in a New Thought gathering. She was an older woman with perfect makeup and hair the color of an orange jujube.

Joyce owned a beautiful gift shop in Swansboro and a lovely home in Cape Carteret. Her children were grown and doing well. She had lots of friends.

There was only one thing she *really* wanted: a church. The closest Unity and Religious Science Churches were too far away for her to make the drive. Her health was iffy and it was too much for her. Even the drive to Jacksonville, NC was a bit of a trek for her.

Her study circle consisted of folks who were young and energetic enough to make the drive to Unity Christ Church in Wilmington. Some were posted at Camp LeJeune and were planning to move away in a year or two.

When she determined that none of them shared her interest in establishing a church, she found another way, which allowed her to stay right where she was.

She made her house into a spiritual center on the first Wednesday of every month. It was perfect for her and it provided a valuable resource in her area for years. When I visited her group to present a workshop, we had a very full house. She had succeeded brilliantly.

What an excellent model of manifestation! Ask, be grateful in advance, let go of the exact form it must come in, be open to inspiration, and act on it. Stay jujube sweet and keep your life filled with laughter. Enjoy your friends and family.

Joyce became both my friend and one of my many mothers. I called her every week. I always asked her what her study group was reading. Once, she sent me a book she liked, **The Power of Appreciation**.

This book had photos illustrating the impact appreciation has on the brain. I was fascinated. I had already noticed that there had usually been *a sense of pleasure* in the back of my head when I have asked and received most quickly and dramatically. Feeling is an important component to creating abundance.

1. Think about a goal with as much happy emotion as you can. Feel it as achieved. Notice the feeling at the back of your head, above where your head meets your neck. Does it feel "lit up" with joy?

2. Keep practicing joy when you think of your goal.

3. Make a Joy Mandala

4. Honor a Joy mentor or friend-in-joy.

There it was again... that "lit up", grateful feeling!

Abundance Triggers

Persistence: Borrowing from Badger

If we are facing in the right direction, all we have to do is keep on walking."
-Buddhist Proverb

Badgers are famous for persistence. One day, I stood with my friend, Anne Davidson, admiring her garden. "I'm dazzled," I exclaimed. "It must take so much care. How ever do you do it?"

"It's easy," she responded. "I work on it fifteen minutes a day, every day."

5. Describe an experience when persistent effort brought you results.

Fred Astaire said that Ginger Rogers was his hardest working dance partner. She would practice for hours until she got a routine as flawless and smooth as she wanted it. Jimi Hendrix was the same way. From the moment that he got his first guitar, it was his constant companion.

6. What do you feel so excited about that you are willing to keep at it?

7. In **Billy Elliot**, when Billy was asked about how he felt when he danced, he described the feeling as "electricity." What does your passion feel like for you?

There is a kind of "electricity" in our bodies. When it flows smoothly, we feel good. When it's blocked, not so good. In the next section, we'll explore triggering good feelings with opening and clearing the flow of vital energy.

Opening up the Flow: Tapping

You can take persistent action towards your worldly goals.

You can take persistent action toward your happiness goals.

You can take persistent action toward removing any resistance you may have toward both action and happiness!

One of the best tools for this is Tapping.

Emotional Freedom Technique, or EFT, is a technique of self-tapping to clear the body/mind of "stuck" energy and old programming. You might think of it as a dynamic blend of self-hypnosis and self-energy work. It was developed by Gary Craig.

Though Tapping is thought of as a modern modality, consider this: one of my clients told me that when her fiancé visited a monastery in Nepal, and the monks used Tapping on him for spiritual healing and upliftment.

Generally, in the West, the thread of the Tapping story really begins with Dr. Roger Calahan, who founded Thought Field Therapy (TFT), and Gary Craig, who studied with Dr. Calahan and then modified and streamlined the technique. EFT is practical, easy and very accessible.

You can go to eftuniverse.com and find helpful information. There is a also link to Gary's revised manual. Since I first learned EFT, Gary has made further tweaks to simplify and improve the technique.

In working with a friend who is an EFT specialist I learned an updated version and some creative adaptations. I also made some of my own adaptations, through working with it on my own and with clients. I'm offering you a short version that is widely in use.

For continued updates on EFT, I recommend going to www.eftuniverse and signing up for the e-newsletter, which is an excellent resource. You can also go to YouTube and see demonstrations of Tapping.

I'm going to outline some basic information about Tapping and then we'll apply it specifically to shifting from lack to abundance consciousness.

Kanta Bosniak

Tapping Points:

Karate Chop   Outside edge of hand on the side near the little finger.

Sore Spot   About midway between your nipple and your shoulder, at the level of your heart, on either side. If on the left side, it will be over your heart. If on the right, it will be the mirror image. I like to use the heart side.

Top of Head   Right in the middle, at the crown.

Eyebrow   On the inside end of your eyebrow (the side closer to your nose)

Outside Eye   Between the outside of your eye and your temple.

Under Eye   Right where you'd put a cucumber slice to diminish puffiness.

Under Nose   Between your nose and your lip, on that little indented place.

Chin   Between your lip and your chin, in that other indented place.

Collarbone   Place your finger on top of your collarbone and run it along from the outside in, toward your throat, till you get to the place where it turns down and makes a little "L." Tap on the inside of that "L."

Under Arm   On your side, several inches below your armpit. If you are a woman, this will be where your bra comes around on the side.

Basic Tapping Technique

This is a good overall technique and can be used anytime, either for immediate concerns as they arise, or for proactive reduction of those concerns. In other words, you might choose to take a few minutes each day to shrink your egoic negativity down to size and reclaim your peace and power. Tapping can be a good addition to your spiritual practice.

Tap with your dominant hand. So, on the setup, you will be tapping with your dominant hand on the Karate Chop Point of your non-dominant hand.

Tap using at least two fingers: your index finger and your middle finger. Some points, like the Karate Chop point or the Top of the Head point are so large that you can use four fingers. Some points, like the eyebrow point, are so small that only two fingers will fit.

Tapping is about clearing. It works with stored material in the energetic system, along the meridians, or pathways of energy throughout the body. It is related to acupuncture and acupressure.

Generally, in New Thought affirmative prayer and in Guided Imagery (which really is extended, highly focused, and personalized New Thought affirmative prayer) we don't use "negative" language. We focus on what we want, not on what we don't want.

Tapping is a little different. It acknowledges the negative that has been buried and running a chronic energetic program. And at the same time it affirms the positive in a strong statement of self-affirmation. The result is clearing of the energetic pattern throughout the body/mind. This phenomenon is like what in hypnosis terms would be called "collapsing an anchor." A strong positive anchor evoked at the same time as a negative anchor weakens the negative anchor to the point that it no longer operates.

Before doing the Set-up, identify the feeling and get it up as high as you can on a scale of 0-10. This is not about basting yourself in negative emotion. It's about moving it out quickly and efficiently. Think of it as a pre-soak.

The purpose of placing the concern on the number scale is really to get a feel for how well this works. It's a teaching, or in this case a self-teaching tool. Once you experience how that number goes down with a round of tapping, the purpose has been served.

The Set-up and Sequence

The Set-up Sentence is constructed to begin the process of collapsing the anchor and the Tapping sequence that follows carries this process throughout the entire system by activating the meridians associated with the points that you tap.

Here's the basic Set-up Sentence:

"Even though I have this _____, I deeply and completely accept myself.

What goes in the blank should be a feeling, not an overly abstract idea. It doesn't matter if your set-up is grammatically correct, either.

What matters is that it means something to **you**. It helps you bring up the feeling and then clear it out.

So, this is too abstract: "Even though I have this tendency to worry about my finances, I deeply and completely accept myself." This is better: "Even though I have this money fear, I deeply and completely accept myself."

You say the Set-up Sentence three times while tapping continuously on the Karate Chop Point OR rubbing in a circular motion on the Sore Spot (over your physical heart).

Then you move on to tapping the Sequence. At each point of the Sequence, you tap at least 7-9 times. Please don't bother counting. It's perfectly OK to tap more than 9 times. And, it's more important to stay focused on the feeling. Toward this end, you say the Reminder Phrase. This is the phrase with which you filled in the blank. In the example above, the Reminder Phrase is "this money fear."

Here are two more examples:

For the Set-up Sentence, "Even though I have this resentment of rich people, I deeply and completely accept myself."

The Reminder Phrase is "this resentment of rich people."

It's OK to experiment with your Basic Set-up. I sometimes use "I deeply love and accept myself, "or "I deeply accept and forgive myself."

You can say the words out loud. You can also choose to **think** them. One round of Set-up followed by Sequence will usually take a level 9 or 10 down to a 5 or 6, sometimes lower. A second round will usually take a level 5 or 6 down to a 0-3.

Basic Shortcut Version

Rate challenge on number scale 0-10.
Setup.
Say Setup sentence "Even though I have this _____, I deeply and completely accept myself," while tapping continuously on the karate chop point or rubbing on the sore spot. Do this 3 times.

Then do the Sequence.
Say reminder phrase + tap at least 7-9 times on these points in this order:
Top of head
Eyebrow   (inside end of eyebrow)
Side of eye
Under Eye
Under nose
Chin (between lip and chin)
Collarbone (below collarbone)
Underarm

Rate number now.

If there is a need to further reduce the number, you can do another round, or as many as you like. Typically, I find that most people do from two or three rounds for most things. Often one is all it takes. Once in a while it may take as many as four.

New Setup
"Even though I still have some of this remaining _____, I deeply and completely accept myself," while tapping continuously on the karate chop point or rubbing on the sore spot.

Do sequence again with new reminder phrase: "This remaining _____."

Rate number now.

Alternate Method

I absolutely love this method. I recommend using it once you've gotten your number down to a four or below. This is because this method contains a cognitive, self-reflective component.

When you experience a strong feeling, it can be difficult to remember that you are the thinker who thought the thought that generated the emotion.

This method reminds you that you are not the victim of the feeling. You are the creator of it. We all have an Observer. It's a part of our mind that is like a mentor to us. We both live our lives and observe our lives. That's how we learn.

However, though we are always connected with our Observer, when we are experiencing strong emotions, we may not be as **aware** of our Observer.

At a four or below, you're more grounded and more in touch with the Observer, that higher, wiser part of you that says, "Hey, you know what? You chose that. Now, you can un-choose it. You can think happier thoughts and generate happier feelings."

This is where you really make shifts into abundance consciousness, using Tapping as an abundance trigger!

The Set-up is very simple: "Even though, _____ I prefer peace." As with the Basic Set-up, it's said three times while tapping on the Karate Chop point OR rubbing on the Sore Spot.

Then, tap the Sequence, alternating with the Problem Reminder Phrase and the Solution Reminder Phrase. You start with the Problem and end with the Solution.

The following is an example:

Rate number (4 or below).
Setup.

Say setup sentence "Even though I have this _____, I prefer peace," while tapping continuously on the karate chop point or rubbing on the sore spot. Do this 3 times.

Then do the Sequence, tapping at least 7-9 times at each point, and inserting what you want to clear away in place of the (problem).

Say "this (problem)" and tap at Top of Head
Say "I prefer peace" and tap at Eyebrow (inside end of eyebrow)
Say "this (problem)" and tap at Side of Eye
Say "I prefer peace" and tap at Under Eye
Say "this (problem)"and tap at Under Nose
Say "I prefer peace" and tap at Chin (between lip and chin)
Say "this (problem)" Collarbone (below collarbone)
Say "I prefer peace" and tap at Underarm

Rate number now. Most people get to 0-1 after this round. It's elegant!

8. Review the Basic Method. Write some basic Tapping set-ups that are most relevant for you, and Tap on them.

9. Once you get your level down to 4 or below, do some the Basic way and try the Alternate Method on some of them.

10. Periodically, check in with yourself and try new Set-ups, as you explore abundance consciousness and find pockets of resistance to dissolve.

Bodywork

EFT is a wonderful modality that you can do yourself anytime you want to shift your state. I think it's also an important part of self-care and spiritual development to utilize bodywork.

Massage, Energy Work, Acupuncture and Chiropractic can all be abundance triggers. They are wonderful ways to feel good and to clear energetic blocks. They also complement and enhance the releasing work you do in your

Meditation and/or in Guided Meditation with a spiritual coach, or in some other way.

If you're not already incorporating bodywork into your life, you might enjoy researching talented practitioners in your area.

This is always good for opening up conversation. People love to refer great bodyworkers and they'll be happy to do so!

11. Allow yourself to be nurtured in a way that suits your needs.

Movement

Many of us spend so much of our time sitting at a desk looking at a screen. Then we go home and look at another screen on our sofa or in our home office.

Too much time in our heads and on our hineys, and we lose vital energy. Movement is an immediate abundance state-shifter. You may have a preference or you might enjoy exploring…

Ecstatic and Aesthetic movement: Dance!

Conscious movement: Yoga, Tai Chi, Qigong

Sports

Working out at the gym or at home, using weight, treadmill, etc.

Outdoor activities like walking, hiking, biking, skiing, swimming

12. What's fun for you? Enjoy some movement today!

13. If you notice resistance, try this Tapping set up: "Even though I don't want to move my body, I deeply and completely accept myself."

14. Check for negative associations with body movement. Does it feel like work or play? What would make it feel more like play?

15. As you add more movement into your life, record shifts in your feeling state.

Self-Soothing

Exercise is a stress-reducing behavior. A walk outside, stroll by the river, connecting with nature…

Consider other forms of relaxation that you can enjoy at home. Reading in bed, a cup of cocoa, lighting a fragrant candle, soaking in the tub, an afternoon nap, creative self-expression...

16. What's relaxing for you?

17. Give yourself permission, and treat yourself.

18. If you notice resistance to relaxation, try this Tapping Set-up: "Even though I don't want to relax, I deeply and completely accept myself."

Grooming and Beauty Care

When we see someone who's not taking care of him or herself, we instinctively wonder what's going on. Personal grooming or the lack thereof is one of the many non-verbal signals we send as to the state of our well-being.

As we send these signals out to others, we also send them to ourselves. So, taking good care of yourself can be a powerful and immediate state shifter. These actions say "I love myself."

19. Take a self-care action or treat yourself to a haircut, manicure or other service, and observe how this shifts your state.

20. What did you notice?

Chapter 7

Sounds Good

Make a joyful noise unto the Lord all ye lands.
Serve the Lord with gladness.
                  -Psalm 100

What sounds like abundance to you? What, when you hear it, triggers happy feelings or feelings of luxury? The voice of your Beloved? The laughter of your child? The sound of trumpets? The subtle rustle of paper money? Spring peepers on a country night? The roar of a jet, as you take off for new adventures?

1. List 8 of your favorite sound triggers for abundance.

2. Use your triggers anytime you want to put yourself into abundance consciousness.

We use sound to trigger desired states without even thinking about it. Music has a language. We put on lively music for working out or cleaning the house. Slow it down and add violins for the emotional side of romance, saxophones and plenty of bass for the joyous, physical, fun side. Flutes bring us up the chakras, drums ground us. Full spectrum music moves us...fully. And consider the human voice...

The hot, soaring voice of Chaka Kahn. The cool musky voice of Diana Krall. Both jazzy; so different! Gregorian chant or chants of India can carry us right into a deep trance. And what about Tuva overtone singers, who can sing more than one tone at the same time? Listen to a concert of Tibetan Buddhist monks chanting in impossibly low chords, and chances are, you'll go right into a deep state of eyes-open meditation. You may, as I did, feel the vibration in your back.

I felt it going down my spine all the way from the back of my neck to my root chakra!

3. List some vocalists or instrumental artists whose music revs you up...

4. Relaxes you...

5. Makes you feel happy...

6. Loving...

7. Sexy...

8. Creative...

9. Spiritual...

10. Sleepy...

They're Playing My Song

"I celebrate myself and sing myself."
-Walt Whitman

In spiritual love poetry, such as the work of Rumi, the Beloved might be a lover, and really is God. Much of popular music could be heard this way, too.

1. Listen to your favorite (happy) love song as a message from you to your Higher Self.

2. Listen again as a message from your Higher Self to you.

3. What are the love songs that could work on a spiritual level that most inspire you?

4. Write a verse of a happy love poem to God.

5. Write one to yourself, celebrating and loving yourself.

Music of the Spheres: Good Vibrations and Resonance

I've had many interesting experiences with vibration, in and outside of my work. Once, I attended a seminar on energy healing instruments in New York City. Some of these instruments are handheld and some are flat and can be mounted on a wall. I sat in the chair provided and put both hands on the wall instrument.

I literally felt a pulsating energy come through my hands, down my arms, and into my body. There was a visual of streaming colored lights that accompanied the bodily sensation. It is not necessary to use a healing instrument to experience the benefits of "good vibrations."

I've had similar experiences in meditations, though the streaming light and pulsating energy did not come through the hands. It poured into the entire body/mind. I could say it was pleasurable, but that word does not begin to come close to the wonder and delight I felt.

When I facilitate a Guided Meditation, it is not only the words that guide the listener into his or her own center of Peace. I go into a state of higher awareness and changes occur in the tone and overall sound of my voice. I've even occasionally heard something that sounds almost like a chord.

Thought (affirmative prayer or "spiritual suggestion") changes vibration. Slow down the vibration, using this same spiritually focused thought, and a resonance is created.

Thoughts come into harmonious alignment with higher consciousness. We are in our God-nature. Our limited thinking falls away. Potential opens up. The Holy Spirit works in the situation, whatever it may be.

I speak the words the client wants to hear in terms of affirmative prayer. That certainly plays a part. And I have also had experiences which have led me to believe that words do not necessarily need to be spoken.

The thought itself has a vibration and that vibration, like the energy of Reiki, can be heard across oceans and time zones.

Dr. Emotos's research, which I previously mentioned, bears this out. Water exposed to prayer, and silent, written words, like that exposed to positive spoken words and uplifting music, became clearer, less polluted and in its frozen state, showed more beautiful and better organized crystalline structures.

> *Words are also seeds, and when dropped into the*
> *invisible spiritual substance, they grow and bring*
> *forth after their kind.*
> *-Charles Fillmore*

Changing Self-Talk:
From Instant Boomerang to Instant Boost

Of course words affect your mind and mood as well. They're going to be triggers for good or for ill. So why not use them to your advantage? Your self-talk, the unspoken sound, or vibratory thought in your head influences your state of being. Once you begin becoming aware of your own inner dialogue, it's easier to change it.

6. Listen to your inner dialogue. If you notice self-criticism, cancel it and replace it with a self-affirming statement.

7. Write the affirmation in your journal.

Affirmations and Denials

When you have been carrying around an ego-driven lie for a long time, it can be useful to use denial as a tool. Look right at the ego and call it a liar. When you look right at the lie in the light of compassion, much of it will dissolve immediately.

Remember as you do this to call in even bigger help. The Holy Spirit, Christ Consciousness, your Higher Power (however you choose to think of it) will work within you to (literally!) change your mind.

Deny, and then affirm. Always move your energy away from what you don't want and into what you want…away from what you aren't into what you are.

Let the last words you speak to yourself in any inner conversation leave a delicious taste in your mouth and mind.

Rolling Marquees and Sticky Notes

Affirmations can be spoken, sung, or written. Writing them down creates an extremely potent trigger. When they are written, they serve as auditory, kinesthetic and visual anchors. You subvocalize it as you write it and as you read it. Your get your body involved as you write. And when you read it, it serves as a visual anchor. You might consider playing with different ways to use written anchors, such as placing affirmative rolling marquees or virtual sticky notes on your computer's desktop, or posting actual sticky notes anywhere you like.

Chapter 8

You Who Sit on my Eyelids

*"What I have tried to point to is art as inspiration-
art which activates the dynamics of hope in a culture
saturated with despair, through images that
empower the collective unconscious"*
  - *Suzi Gabik*

You are That Beauty Which Shines From Within.

What looks like abundance to you? What, when you see it, triggers happy feelings or feelings of luxury? A full fruit basket? A dozen long-stemmed roses? A sleeping puppy? A new pair of shoes?

1. List 8 of your favorite visual triggers for abundance.

2. Use your triggers anytime you want to put yourself into abundance consciousness.

Behold!

In my yoga teacher days, I was captivated by a line of imagery in a Sanskrit chant of appreciation to the Divine. The song addresses God in various ways, one of which is "You Who Sit on My Eyelids."

Isn't that amazing poetry? How light and gentle the Presence must be to perch in such a sensitive spot. So subtle, that one might forget to realize that one is seeing God everywhere one looks...God in all faces...God in all situations and in all undertakings with which we may be involved.

Abundance Triggers

There are several levels of lessons one may learn in the yoga society to which I belonged. However, it is said that the first and the second are the most important, and that if practiced diligently and with devotion to God, they are sufficient tools for reaching Enlightenment.

The first lesson is one of self-identification with Spirit. The second is identification of everything else as Spirit. In other words, God is all there is. God is in the problems we face, which are our soul lessons. God is in the overcoming of our challenges and in our successes.

It is this second lesson that the eyelid imagery references. When all we see is Maya (illusion), eternal spirit in physical drag, then Love is the only choice that makes any sense. When relating to one's brother or sister, it is not "there, but for the grace of God go I; it's there go I."

When relating to one's life process and each moment-to-moment experience, there is cause for gratitude. Even doing your taxes can be an opportunity to trigger joy and gratitude. Last year, as I played with piles of paper, in a momentary break from left brain activity, I suddenly saw the receipts and paper piles as a beautiful mess. Here's the journal entry:

Paper Flowers

Islands of tiny paper pieces float on my office carpet. Each bears witness to a life I love. Toll receipts: Evidence of peaceful, prosperous pilgrimages to city, mountain, more, heart-connected journeys home.

Slips for pink and golden lilies to delight the visitor in the comfy chair

and call her in to dreamtime landscapes. For books, my old friends, full of wisdom beyond time and space, for the shipping companies and the postal service...

Happy debris, like trimmed-off lower leaves, sending bouquets of words and sounds to relax, inspire and heal. Phone and internet, connecting me with clients far and wide... with family, friends, with you.

At the end of the day I'll collect these piles of petals, once juicy experiences, now dried except in grateful memory, put them in the attic box, and return to my downstairs life.

Today, I'll buy more flowers.

3. Look around you at your physical environment. What do you see? What experiences do those images and objects symbolize for you? Write a gratitude poem.

A Client Responds to Beauty

What, then, is beauty? It is a symbol. As Coco Chanel once said, "Beauty is never anything but a reflection of the heart." We see the beauty inside and behind the painting, the film, the written word, art in any form.

Several years ago, a woman I'll call Cynthia came to my old holistic center, which also doubled as a gallery of my spiritual art. She worked her way through the lobby and waiting room, up the stairs, along a hallway and into my interview room.

All of the spaces she moved through were filled with vibrant visionary folk art paintings, icons, mandalas, hearts and other imagery of love and inspiration.

She sat down on the leather chair and glanced across the room at the fresh flowers and candles. We talked a while. Then, I asked her if she had decided to work with me. Was she ready to stop smoking?

"Oh yes!" she responded. "I made up my mind right away, because of how you have it set up. I felt completely comfortable here."

"Set up?" I said, puzzled.

"The art. All of it."

The non-verbal communication had been clearly sent and received though the environmental objects, images and spatial arrangements. Visual abundance triggers, all.

The messages I wanted to send my visitors: You matter. You are precious. You are beautiful. You are loved. You are Spirit. You can accomplish your goals.

You can send yourself messages too, visual reminders of your worth, your Divine heritage ….reminders to have fun, and to rest. You can place visual triggers in your home or office to stay on track to achieve your goals… and reminders that you are receiving all the help you need.

Power Objects and Images as Reminders

You probably have some of these visual reminders already, in your home, your workplace, and even in your car. Most of us have an innate understanding that we can use objects as triggers and we do it all the time.

We use photos to remember that we are loved and to evoke the love we feel. We use diplomas, certificates of achievement, and awards to remind ourselves that we're smart and competent. They help us realize that just as we have accomplished goals in the past, so we can accomplish our present ones.

Eyes on the Prize

We use images and objects as self-coaching tools, to help us move through the challenges we may experience as we work toward out goals.

For example, skinny pictures of ourselves on the fridge help us stay on track while we're reshaping our bodies. Images and objects can even serve to help us meet our spiritual goals.

We can also use them to help us interrupt unwanted patterns like worry or anger and anchor those we desire, like confidence and serenity. Many people place a framed Serenity Prayer in their home for this purpose, or they have recovery slogans on the bumpers of their car.

I have a dear friend who works as an investment counselor. Because she values peace and wants to stay grounded, regardless of her fast-paced job, she uses images of the turtle.

Turtle Medicine says, "Even when you must move quickly in your life, deliberate well and wisely. Keep an inner stillness. Stay grounded and peaceful, and remember your spiritual foundation."

In his work with patients, Swiss psychiatrist Carl Jung found that his patients, when asked to draw, made the same images, regardless of age, gender, country of origin and background. Some are Sun, Moon, Man, Woman, Child, Tree of Life and Mandala. These and other archetypal images make up a symbolic language of the soul.

In divination, images can be used for ***receiving*** information from inner guidance. For example, in Tarot, Wands or Rods signify work, enterprise and growth.

There are divination cards for retrieving one's "power animal," which represents qualities to develop and utilize. These may be symbolized by animals, birds, insects and reptiles. Angel and Goddess cards are for accessing archetypal wisdom.

Images and objects may have cross cultural meaning and they may also be more personal. The elephant signifies good fortune and money in multiple cultures. In India, it shows up as Ganesha, the elephant God, that aspect of the Divine which removes obstacles and brings success.

Among the many cross-cultural symbols of abundance are the full cup or pitcher, the cornucopia, fruits, vegetables, and flowers, grains, eggs, seeds, and images of the Divine Feminine in all its forms: statuary, baskets and bowls, shells, textiles, spheres, circles, hearts and mandalas, mothers, pregnant women, and plants that are full and lush.

A personal power object or image can be any symbol that has meaning for you or to which you assign meaning. It can be an object you link to a job or career goal, an image of a place you want to visit, or whatever calls to you.

For triggering abundance consciousness, I recommend ***sending*** information to your creative team: your Subconscious and your Superconscious Mind, by selecting images and objects that signify your goals and placing them where you will see them often. It will help you stay focused, strengthen your intention and amplify the power of your emotions.

One of my closest friends used this principle. After her children were grown and many years of post-divorce singlehood, she decided she wanted love in her life again. She placed hearts all over her house.

Very shortly afterward, she met someone wonderful, handsome, mega-talented, kind, and smart, who gets her amazing sense of humor and adores her. They have been married for many years now. I think their happiness serves as a youth serum, because they both look at least 10 years younger than their "calendar" ages.

Consider your present dreams and goals. What objects or images might serve as abundance triggers for your...

4. Health and Vitality

5. Finances

6. Career

7. Relationships

8. Creativity

9. Spirituality

10. When you go to sleep at night, ask your inner guidance for just the right symbolic triggers for you.

11. In the morning, record any images you may have received.

12. Find objects or images that match what you retrieved as closely as possible and place them in your environment.

If you would like a full Guided Imagery for power object retrieval, you can use the companion CD to this book, entitled **Abundance Triggers: A Journey of Self Discovery.** You can find it on Amazon or through my website.

Abundance Triggers

The Divine Feminine

"Just as God has been from the beginning so Spirit substance has been from the beginning. This substance is in fact the Mother side of God, the feminine element in God's nature. It is the universal medium in which we plant all ideas of supply and support."

-Charles Fillmore

Images and objects which represent the Divine Feminine are particularly important abundance triggers. Not only do they represent abundance directly, they also represent both the unconditional love that we feel from God that allows us ask for and to receive our good and the love that we have for ourselves that allows us to receive it.

The Divine Masculine

Receiving resources is a beginning. We must connect with inner illumination and take action to use our talents. The Divine Masculine represents inspiration, the activating principle within ourselves and the qualities related to engaging in the world: discernment, strategy, courage, determination, focus, and follow-through.

It also represents these same qualities as applied to spiritual work. The sword or dagger, for example, is a symbol of cutting through fear, doubt and other egoic negativity. Some other images of the Masculine are the sky, sun, stars, rods, scepters, candles, fire, metallic objects, bulls, spires, tall buildings, tall trees and plants that have a spired or spiky appearance.

Abundance Triggers

Color Me Wealthy

Green, purple and gold are commonly known as abundance colors. I think it's also useful to make friends with red, orange and yellow, the colors of the first three chakras. These are all "Masculine," active colors. They're grounding and they inspire constructive action and the energy to undertake it. It is important to balance dreaming with action!

Religious Symbols

Cross, Medicine Wheel, Star of David, Pentagram, Sacred Spiral, Shri Yantra, Mandalas and more...some symbols have exoteric accepted religious meaning and esoteric, spiritual or metaphysical meaning.

13. What symbols please and inspire you?

14. What do they mean to you?

The Empty Vessel

It is not my purpose in this book to provide a complete dictionary of symbols. There are ample books on that subject and oodles of information at the touch of your keypad.

For our purpose here, it's less important to study accepted meanings of images than it is to access and use those images that are meaningful **to you**. After all, if you're using symbols as a way of communication between parts of yourself, it makes sense to use language that you prefer, in your own dialect!

However, there's one more power object I want to include, because of its importance in the manifestation cycle. And that's the empty vessel.

The empty vessel can be a cup, a chalice or a bowl. The larger, more open shape of a ceramic bowl is especially appropriate to fully convey the meaning of this symbol of receptivity. The open vessel may be used to invite prosperity. It may also be a request for guidance. It says, "I'm ready to listen now. What's my next step?"

I left this symbol for the end of the section because it represents what comes at the end of a creative cycle and before the beginning of the next. It is the space between the breaths.

In our culture, we are so geared to produce that our productivity suffers. One must leave open spaces for rest and inspiration. Doing absolutely nothing when it's time to rest is as important a part of the creative cycle as taking action when it's time to act.

The open vessel is a feminine symbol. For our culture to meet its full creative potential, we must right the balance which has skewed to value the material over the value of human life and well-being. When we are open and receptive we get our best ideas and it's going to take fresh new thinking to solve the problems that face our world family and the Sacred Space we call home.

Abundance Triggers

I wrote the following prayer poem ten years ago. It was originally published in SageWoman Magazine. I have performed it at Omega Institute's Café with dance, didgeridoo and drums, at the Association of Research and Enlightenment with music and dance, and at Unity Churches, with various sorts of accompaniment.

Sacred Space

We call on the Mother.

Come, be with us, help us remember you

in the Sacred Space.

We celebrate your coming out of exile, from banishment that we have created in our hearts for you,

who are our heart.

We have been rended from our roots, Mother,

a nation of bean-counters who have forgotten

where the beans come from.

We send the prayer to the four directions.

We send the prayer to the earth and sky.

Wholeness is now, in me, in you, in us.

Let it be so.

Let me feel the place where stars and soil connect:

my feet. And let my walking be in rhythm with your heartbeat, which is my heartbeat.

We have been splintered from ourselves, Mother.

A nation of people who despise women, elders, children

is a broken family. Let us be healed.

Let me love my learning as dearly as my knowing,

my sensing as clearly as my thinking,

my resting as fully as my work.

Let me choose to do the work that resonates with my soul,

which is your soul.

We have been out of sync with our own lungs,

Trying only to breathe out:

doing, making, working

or only in:

getting, taking, hoarding

has left us gasping for air.

Let us merge with the breath

which is your breath.

Breathe into us, until we know that we are one breath.

Fill our souls, until we know that we are one soul.

Walk with us, until we know that all our movement is one dance,

moving ever

in Sacred Space.

15. Breathe deeply and allow some space between your breaths.

16. Increase and savor your rest time!

17. Visualization: In a standing position, feel your feet connect with the earth. Imagine sending roots down into the earth, way down deep, connecting with the earth electrically. Imagine drawing up some green, abundant energy from the earth. Let it circulate through your body, healing and revitalizing you.

    When you're ready, you can mentally dissolve the roots and come back, feeling relaxed and refreshed.

Creating Sacred Space: Personal Shrines and Altars

"The images or ideas we entertain are the patterns upon which we build our world and all the things in it."
- Charles Fillmore

Individual focal objects represent ideas. When we put these ideas together in a cohesive and meaningful way, we have a **pattern.** A powerful pattern can propel us forward and sustain our energy and focus for months, years, even a lifetime.

The creative confluence of the ideas is like lovers coming together. Two powerfully linked ideas give birth to others. They generate corollaries.

Altars are the ground for these visual patterns. An altar can be as simple as a vase of flowers in between two candles. Or, it can be quite complex. It can be peaceful, energetic, ethereal, campy …whatever best expresses the message you want to communicate to yourself and to God and suits your style.

Like a haiku, it can be spare. Like a film or novel, it can have an overarching theme and vignettes that illustrate that theme in various ways.

There are some really interesting altars in Kay Turner's book, **Beautiful Necessity: The Art and Meaning of Women's Altars**, including a couple of by my friend Diane Porter Goff and myself, made when we were doing altar installation art together.

You can create altars on any surface: On your bureau, your desk, the top of your computer, the dashboard of your car, your dining room table…

You can find altar supplies everywhere! Natural and found objects, knickknacks and curios, crystals and statuary, live plants and dried flowers…

18. To evoke a feeling of connection with nature, play with an asymmetrical arrangement (think Asian).

19. To evoke a feeling of order and balance, play with a symmetrical pattern (think church).

Abundance Triggers

Portrait and Landscape

Artistically, symmetrical altars might be likened to portraits. We are are symmetrical in our bodily design. Symmetry draws the eyes to the center and take us inwards, creating a sense of peace. There is a ritualistic formality about these altars that leads us toward feelings of transcendence.

It can be fun to play with creating symmetry and balance with somewhat unmatching elements. The more exactly matching each side of center, the heavier, more "solid" and potentially dull may be the result. You can infuse your symmetrical shrine with interest by adding slight variations. It if pleases you, see how far you can go with this and still maintain the impression of symmetry. This can be a very enjoyable creative experiment.

Asymmetrical altars might be compared to landscape art and the natural world. In fact, they can trigger good feelings instantly, because they evoke our love of nature, like a visual walk in the woods or stroll on the beach. Their elegance is casual and earthy.

They can be studied exercises, or assembled in a seemingly mindless moment. Either way, the most effective designs will seem spacious and spontaneous. These shrines are slices of the big picture, fleeting glimpses.

Unlike symmetrical altars, they don't **depict** order. Rather, they **subtly imply** the order of that Oneness of which they are a part. Even in the asymmetrical, there is Divine Order, just as in seemingly random moments, there is purpose that becomes evident with later reflection.

In either form, altars evoke appreciation for the beauty in the whole... and in the wholeness inside each apparent part. Paradoxically, in altars as well as any sacred art, the symbols of things represent and subconsciously suggest the limitlessness of no-thing, formlessness, eternal Spirit.

Meanwhile, back in the happy dream, we dig in the dirt and we are nourished...

Garden Sanctuaries

One "surface" you can use for altars is the soil. You get the multiple blessing of exercise, fresh air and sunshine and creating beauty! Every stage of gardening is an abundance trigger with its own metaphorical meaning for the stages of manifestation.

20. As you cultivate the soil, open yourself to new ideas.

21. As you prepare the boundary or retaining walls for the bed, focus your intention on a primary goal.

22. As you sew seeds, invest in this goal.

23. As you nourish the plant babies, bless your project.

24. As you weed, let go of limiting ideas and release negative emotions.

25. As your plants fruit and flower, enjoy your success.

26. As you harvest, give thanks for your accomplishment.

27. Garden altars can be quite orderly or relatively wild and (at least seemingly) unstudied. Observe some formal and informal gardens. What do you like about each?

Play!

Magnetboards, sandtrays, dollmaking, visionary art, wearable art and collage are all great ways to play with power objects, images and archetypes.

As with altarmaking, these are all ways you can communicate with your inner being and Higher Self with all of these modalities, while you're having fun expressing your creativity at the same time. I love the work of Seena Frost, who wrote **Soul Collage** and developed the related workshops.

I teach workshops in Treasure Maps (also known as Vision Boards), a way to clarify intention and focus energy on your goals. And I love making Wearable Art for both creative expression and as an abundance trigger.

28. Treasure Map: Make a collage, using pictures from magazines and glue stick. Choose of images that please you, that represent what you most enjoy about life, what you like about yourself what you want to create, your dreams and goals. If you wish to include cutout words, that's fine too. Place it where you'll see it often.

Your Body as an Altar:
Prayers to Wear

People have worn spiritual adornments throughout human history. Priestly and shamanic garments, ceremonial face-painting, tattoos, body piercings, tefillin, turbans, veils and special hats, crosses, yantras, and rings...the sanyasi's orange robes...the white wedding dress, bindis, crucifixes, tokens and talismans...

Changes in dress and adornment signify important life changes. The adoption of religious clothing, head shavings, the first facial hair of an adolescent boy or a girl's first brassiere, high heels and lipstick.

Even changes that are supposed to be sad can inspire adornment reframes as abundance triggers, if you're awake and using your challenges as spiritual rocket fuel.

Ask any woman, and chances are she's sported a "breakup haircut" sometime in her life and perhaps, with the removal of a ring, she celebrated freedom, release and reaffirmation of her personal identity. Chemo baldness invites the exploration of an even lusher and more potent inner goddess that one brings forward into survivorship.

29. What changes in your look marked changes in your life?

30. When have you used a change as an empowerment trigger?

31. A self-esteem trigger?

32. A sexual attractiveness trigger?

33. A prosperity trigger?

Abundance Triggers R US

I once saw an short documentary about Madonna made during her ***Confessions on a Dance Floor*** tour. During a rehearsal break, a Frenchman said to her, "J'aime l'art. I like art."

Madonna responded, "Je suis l'art. I am the art."

And so are you. How you costume yourself can become a conscious act that works side-by-side with your developing self-awareness. Your choices will be personal. You are the one who best knows your heart, and it is your heart that is reflected in your costume choices.

Any list I can offer is only for the purpose of providing a catalyst for your own creative discoveries and expression. I trust you will understand then, as for that reason... and because as bona fide spiritual fashionista, I simply can't resist, I offer you the following sampling of suggestions for wearable abundance triggers. Some of the many possibilities that await you in the Infinite walk-in closet.

Pearls and pink...Unconditional love, self-acceptance, friendship.

Feathers...freedom

Earth colors...Financial grounding, wealth, practicality, authenticity.

Fire Colors...Action, desire, energy. Doing what's there to be done by you!

Turquoise...Abundance in all forms, connection to the earth. And, it looks good on everybody!

Blue...Releasing negativity, protection from negative influences, confidence, Archangel Michael.

Green...Healing, vitality, productivity, money. Go!

Light Blue...Self expression, carrying out creative plans and goals. Air and Sky (Thought, Limitlessness).

Dark, indigo blue...intuition, clairvoyance, guidance.

Purple...transformation, forgiveness, prosperity, depth, integrity.

Gold and Silver...luxury, opulence, unlimited abundance, party time!

White...purity, joy, innocence, spaghetti and salsa are not on the menu.

Black...the all-purpose color. Simplicity, sophistication, receptivity, channeling your Inner Beatnik or New Yorker.

No makeup…Authenticity, sincerity, "I want to be liked for me," self-acceptance.

Makeup. Embracing life, sexuality, The Divine Lila; it's theater, baby!

34. Write your own list of favorite looks and ones you might like to play with.

Chapter 9

Prayer & Meditation

Prayer prepares the way for the Meditation, which is a more advanced version of prayer. You might say that meditation is deep, full-tilt, all lights blazing prayer.

Prayer affirms. Meditation is the experience of what was affirmed. Prayer is about becoming one with Source. Meditation IS that union with Source.

As with courtship and lovemaking, there are words in the beginning. Then there is only one phrase, "I love you." Then, words drop away and there is only the bliss of love.

Prayer is the courtship. When meditation begins with the mantra, that is like the lover focusing his attention. The love phrase is all the lover cares about as he declares his all-consuming desire for the Beloved. Then, bliss takes over and the mantra drops away. There is only ecstatic union.

Prayer

"The gift of mental power comes from God, Divine Being, and if we concentrate our minds on that truth, we become in tune with this great power."
-Nikola Tesla

Prayer affirms functional love and connection, not the needy pretense of love that is really desperate begging. The love and connection are already there. In prayer, we remind ourselves of our oneness. We seek first that remembering. Then, all things flow naturally.

When we ask for what we need and desire, we are really reminding ourselves that our Source supplies these in abundance. We ask, we release the request, we give thanks. Real thanks, not the polite perfunctory kind.

Putting ourselves into a state of joyous appreciation is an essential part of co-creation.

Sometimes, it takes some self-empathy to even begin to pray. It's always OK to start where you are. In my book**, Surviving Cancer and Other Tough Stuff**, I've identified twelve stages in what I call the Becoming Process.

In any transformation, we go through these stages. In our lives, we go through this process many times as we learn and grow. Each new level of awareness brings us to Joy.

Then, we rest a while, until we're ready for a new growth spurt. We usually know we're ready because we feel restless, a little antsy. This sense of malaise indicates our readiness to prepare our minds for more.

We first consider the "more" with some resistance. The old brain resists change. And yet, by using the abundance triggers of prayer and meditation along with our other tools, we gain the courage to move forward.

The following prayer moves through the stages of Becoming all the way to Joy.

Contemplation

Holy Spirit, this dream of mine feels like a prison.

My suffering is beginning to bore me.

Do I need this fear? This doubt? This rage and sadness?

These imaginary bars? I don't think so.

If I'm going to dream

It might as well be happy.

Deep in my being, I know You are there

Beloved, nudge me, please.

Touch me ever so gently on my cheek.

Breathe on my forehead.

Show me beauty in my dreams and in my blessed awakenings.

Acknowledgement

God, I am Yours.

I acknowledge you as my Source.

I also acknowledge the errors of my ego's limited thinking and illusions.

I know how little this world of illusion really matters,

And yet, I am beginning to notice the more I enjoy the gifts of life,

The more I see how it was only ego, which placed such high value on things, which kept these things from me!

It said: "seek" and yet it could never find. It said, "have" and yet it could never enjoy. It said "hold on tightly" and threw away or choked the life out of the things it pretended to desire.

No matter. Even though I realize that my thoughts are out of alignment with who I really am, I am now willing to invite you in. Come into my thoughts, Holy Spirit.

Surrender

I give my mind and heart to you. I know that Love is all there is.

Connection

And I choose Love.

Desire

Love calls me from my innermost being.

Self-Evaluation

It removes the obstacles to itself.

I see myself with new eyes.

I see the walls my ego has erected

I hear the falseness of the mind chatter

I feel the emptiness of the nothing from which came my self-denial.

I realize the court I created and the jury I swore in and the sentence my imaginary judge imposed upon me have no real authority.

I understand the erroneous punishment is mine to pardon.

Responsibility

Holy Spirit, I invite you

Work in my mind.

Lift up my thoughts.

Show me what to do

Moment to moment.

So that I may do what is there to be done by me.

So that I may drink the nectar of your sweetness.

I fill the cup and drink. I pour the cup for my beloveds, too.

You are my One true Love and still,

There is a place for special relationships.

Even with my human self. Yes, even that. It is good to love myself, even as I love my human family and as I love You.

It is good to enjoy. It is good to savor. It is good to dance and sing. It is good to bless and to prosper.

And so, I do.

Each celebration in this world of dreams

Teaches me to dream bigger and brighter.

Acceptance & Forgiveness

Each miracle of forgiveness of myself and those I loved and those for whom I held resentment gives me new permission...

Release

To let go of all that is not Love.

Reframing

To see and hear and feel and know that there is only Love. That all my dark imaginings were but lessons of forgiving

Lessons that opened my heart to You

That tore down the prison walls

That gave sweet abundance to my dream.

Where there was lack, there now is plenty.

Where there was isolation, there now is heart connection

Where there was struggle, there now is ease

Where there was conflict, there now is peace.

You awakened me

And helped me remember who I really am.

Your son, your daughter, your beloved, You,

Holy Spirit, You.

Gratitude

Thank You!

Joy

I love you!

Meditation:
The Ultimate Abundance Trigger

I've been teaching Meditation for over forty years, so if you want an expert, here you go. However, while some instruction can be useful, you don't really need an outside authority to judge the success of your practice, and an inner one is also beside the point.

You are in charge of your spiritual life, and you are a natural meditator! Meditation is easy, natural and there's not one "right way." So please let yourself off the hook, right now!

Easy Does it!

Just as prayer may begin with some resistance in the Contemplation stage, so Meditation may also launch from wherever you are. It is like the lotus flower that rises from the mud. Let yourself rise up free of self-consciousness, free of apology.

You do not have to work at creating perfection in your Meditation. The perfection is already there. Relax! You are formless and eternal Spirit.

Your human dream needs no perfection. There is no perfection in human life. Trying to be perfect is fruitless, distracting and exhausting, not to mention boring.

Bogus perfection is like a matchy-matchy outfit or decorated-by-the books living room. In meditation, as with any art form, it's the little surprise that keeps the spice in things. Stay open. That stray thought may be the answer to a prayer, or an inspiration!

People often say to me, "I try to meditate, but I have thoughts."

And I say, "Congratulations! You're human."

They say, "I try to meditate, but after a while, I fall asleep."

And I say, "And that's a bad thing because?...Meditation is a wonderful way to fall asleep. Enjoy it!"

You might consider your expectations of yourself. If you have a life and you want to be engaged in it, then consider sitting for just a few minutes to start with and work up to whatever length of time makes sense for you.

Fifteen minutes twice a day or half an hour once daily is plenty. More is fine, too, if you can keep it in balance with an active and fully-engaged life. It's important not to spend too much time "in your head."

One of the simplest and most natural ways to meditate is first thing in the morning, before you get up and last thing at night, before you go to sleep.

Research has shown that done regularly, meditation helps the brain and body. It promotes mental clarity and happy mood, too.

If you want to stay awake, you'll have an easier time using a sitting posture. If you want to use meditation as a prelude to sleep, the lying-down posture is ideal. Either way (and even if you drift off while sitting) you will get a benefit.

Basic Meditation

This is a basic version of the traditional Eastern-style meditation that has been done for thousands of years. It is not necessary to sit in a full lotus posture, with your feet pulled up and sitting on top of your calves.

When I do this type of meditation, I either sit in a chair or I sit on the floor in a half-lotus, my left foot up over my right calf, because that is what is most comfortable for me.

If you are more comfortable sitting in the usual cross-legged position, that's fine. This floor position will work prior to surgery and after you're healed. In between, or if the floor isn't comfortable for you, the gentler positions are a better idea.

It's as easy as A, B, C. The three part process goes like this:

A. **"*Pratyahara*"** which means withdrawing from outer-world orientation and identification with your Divine Source.

B. Focusing your attention on an idea, using breath and an internal sound (mantra) and its meaning.

C. Letting go of thought and mantra and just resting in the Light and Love of God.

Mantra: Meaning and Purpose

Have you ever tried to think of two things at the same time? It's not easy, is it? The mantra is an ideation, usually of two to four syllables, that helps keep you focused on one thought. For this reason, traditionally, it is analogized as a sword, cutting away mental distractions.

The mantra is not just any random couple of words, though. It's chosen to help you concentrate on a particular idea. There are many mantras in traditional Eastern meditation, for contemplation of various spiritual ideas. The main spiritual idea though, and the primary goal of yogis, is about experiencing oneness with God.

So, one of the most popular mantras is Ham So, or "I am That." As you breathe in, think "Ham" (pronounced like Hahng). As you breathe out, think "So." As you continue to say this mantra, it becomes a circle, which is translates to a repetition of the name of God in Western scripture:

I AM THAT I AM.

If you prefer to use English, you might choose "I rest" on the in-breath and "in God" on the out-breath, or some other words of similar meaning that work well with your breathing. Pick something short and simple.

And, of course, if your primary language is something other than English, choose what works for you. I prefer the Sanskrit because I feel more positive "charge" to the words; they have innate energy in them and they more efficiently take me where I want to go, into a feeling of bliss.

Floor-seated method

First, create a sacred space. Ask your partner or family to give you some undisturbed alone time. Light some incense, if you like. Turn off your phone. Sit on the floor with your legs crossed and back straight.

If you wish, you may begin by doing the "Namaste" salutation: holding your hands in prayer position and touching your thumb to your forehead and then to your heart center, in the middle of your chest.

This is a way of greeting your Divine Source and physically affirming your intention to connect with that Source. Then, let your hands rest cupped comfortably in your lap or, if you prefer, palms up on your knees.

Imagine that you are sitting on your own personal little planet (Do you remember the tiny planets in **The Little Prince**?). All your concerns of the day are very distant now. You are present in the moment, noticing your breath. The deep indigo sky is full of sparkling stars. The planet begins to glow underneath you. You can feel it glowing brighter and brighter.

You can feel its energy at the base of your spine, awakening your own spiritual energy. The planet becomes fully luminous and as it does, it disappears. It has transferred all of its energy to the base of your spine, where you have absorbed it.

You are now sitting, fully supported and comfortable, suspended in space. Focus your attention on the very tip of your right big toe.

Begin moving the energy from your toe up through your foot in a focused stream of light, collecting the energy all along the way, up through your right leg, up through your thigh, your hip and all the way to the base of your spine.

Let the energy rest there as a ball of light. It continues to rest there as you focus your attention on the tip of your left big toe. Next, bring the energy up through your foot, your leg, your thigh, all the way to the base of your spine, where it joins the ball of light there.

Begin bringing the energy up through your body. You can imagine it going up your spine or up through a sort of central light column that goes to the top of your head, continuing to gather the energy of your body as it goes.

First, bring it up a few inches to the level of your reproductive organs and let it rest there...now bring it up to your solar plexus and let it rest...to the center of your chest...to your throat...to between your brows...to the top of your head.

You can let it rest there or you can bring it forward in an arc that curves around and down to the tip of your nose. Whichever spot you choose is fine. At that spot, imagine a shining sun-like ball of light and mentally gaze upon it. As you continue to focus on this light, notice your breath.

Now, mentally say the mantra you have chosen in rhythm with your breath. Keep focusing on the sun and your mantra, feeling the meaning of it as you breathe.

Don't worry if you have passing thoughts; just let them pass, and bring your attention back to the image, mantra, and breath.

Imagine that you are breathing yourself into the light and breathing the light into you, joining yourself to the light, resting in it, and letting it fill you with its healing energy.

If you forget to say your mantra as you relax into the light, that's fine. You may enjoy this for ten minutes, twenty or half an hour. Longer, if you wish.

Any time you spend in meditation will benefit you mind, body and spirit. It is especially helpful to meditate twice a day, if only for a short time.

Chair seated method

Similar to the basic method, but shorter and simpler. Sit with your hands cupped in your lap or resting palms up on your knees.

Bring the energy up in flossed streams of light, from the bottoms of both your feet (at the same time), through both your legs, until the energy meets at the base of your spine.

Now bring it up through the other centers as above, ending in the same way.

Lying Down method

This is the same as chair method, but lying down on your back. If you like, you may support you back by placing two or three pillows under your knees.

This is a good way to meditate before rising in the morning and to ease you into sleep at night. It's also great for getting back to sleep if you arise in the night.

Whatever your favorite position for meditation, it can give you a much-needed feeling of groundedness and balance during any stressful time and will help you move from "stress to bless."

1. If you have any previous self-judgments about your ability to Meditate, forgive them. You might imagine them dissolving in light, being drawn up through the top of your head and taken away by angels…whatever works for you.

2. Try a few forms of meditation. What seems most natural to you?

3. Try a few different mantras. What works best for you?

Eyes Open Meditation

Truly, any action can be a meditation with the proper ideation. There are some activities that especially lend themselves to Alpha and even deeper Theta states. Here are some you can explore:

4. Mindful, slow walking
5. Mindful, slow eating
6. Loving, heart-connected sex
7. Driving on the highway or on country roads
8. Connecting with Nature
9. Painting and mandala-making
10. Listening to or making music
11. Weaving, knitting, crochet and other handwork
12. Any creative activity. What's fun for you?
13. Dance
14. Walking, hiking, biking, swimming
15. Any athletic activity
16. Service activities
17. What are your favorites in this list? Add any more that occur to you.

Kanta Bosniak

Abundance Triggers

"Books were my pass to personal freedom." — Oprah Winfrey

Resources
Books

The Dynamic Laws of Prosperity, (and all books by) Catherine Ponder

As a Man Thinketh   James Allen

Think and Grow Rich   Napoleon Hill

The Four Spiritual Laws of Abundance: A Simple Guide to Unlimited Abundance   Edwene Gaines

A Course in Miracles   Foundation for Inner Peace

It's My Pleasure   Maria Rodale, Maya Rodale

The Mission of Art   Alex Grey

Reenchantment of Art   Suzi Gablik

Concerning The Spiritual in Art   Wassily Kandinsky

Soul Collage   Seena B. Frost

The Abundance Book   John Randolph Price

Ask and It Is Given   Esther and Jerry Hicks

The Power of Appreciation   Noelle C. Nelson, Jeannine Lemare Calaba

You Can Heal Your Life   Louise L. Hay

Animal Speak   Ted Andrews

The Medicine Cards   Jamie Sams, David Carson, Angela C. Werneke

The Power of Myth   Joseph Campbell, Bill Moyers

Pathway to Bliss   Joseph Campbell

Getting The Love You Want   Harville Hendrix, PhD

The Red Book   Carl Gustav Jung

Mandala: Luminous Symbols for Healing   Judith Cornell

Healing Mandalas   Lisa Tenzin-Dolma

Complete Dictionary of Symbols   Jack Tresidder

The Secret Language of Symbols   David Fontana

The Essential Rumi   Rumi, Coleman Barks

Pronoia is the Antidote for Paranoia   Rob Brezsny

Beautiful Necessity: The Art and Meaning of Women's Altars   Kay Turner

Surviving Cancer and Other Tough Stuff: An Illustrated Journal and Workbook for Healthy and Abundant Life   Kanta Bosniak

Lose Weight in Alpha State: Weight Loss as a Joyous Spiritual Journey Kanta Bosniak

CDs

Surviving Cancer: A Sacred Journey for Women   Kanta Bosniak, with music by Joshua Bosniak

Lose Weight in Theta State: Guided Imagery for Weight Loss Kanta Bosniak, with music by Joshua Bosniak

Abundance Triggers: A Journey of Self Discovery   Kanta Bosniak, with music by Joshua Bosniak

Contact

KantaBosniak.com

art4spirit@yahoo.com

Tell me your abundance stories!

Book a Coaching & Guided Imagery session!

Invite me to speak at your church or spiritual center!

Reviews for Abundance Triggers
(formerly Sacred Space) Workshops

I recommend you most highly to Unity Churches and Centers of Spiritual Living in search of a dynamic, articulate and entertaining Guest Minister as well as talented and engaging workshop presenter. Thank you so very much for your wonderful presentations and presence at Spirit of Unity Church.

The congregation was delighted, as was I. I have heard great feedback. It's been a few years since your wonderful Sacred Space workshop for my congregation, when you delighted us and inspired us to create personal sanctuaries.

Please know that your impact was felt then, and now. You share deeply and generously of your wisdom and creativity and I know that God will bless you abundantly for your open heart. We hope you will come back soon.

With Deepest Gratitude,

Rev. Alicia-Leslie
Minister, Spirit of Unity Church

The experience was inspiring...I highly recommend the workshop."

Joan Compton
Board of Trustees, Unity in Greensboro

"The altar Kanta created with the participants was beautiful and the group sharing of things to release and things to manifest was a powerful experience...

...I recommend [this workshop] to any Unity Church or other group that is seeking to explore creativity as it relates to Spirit (as indeed all creativity does) or to deepen the connection with the Divine in the daily life of its members."

Barbara Pollack
Events Coordinator, Crystal Coast Unity

"If art is the soul of life, then Kanta is a beautiful rainbow. This became even more evident to me during the altar making workshop led by Kanta the day after her show opened at Urban Artware…The altarmaking workshop through its magical blending of art, spirituality, and connection with others helped me refocus and get back on track.

As I write this I am fully aware that there is no way I can possibly express in words what knowing Kanta and experiencing one of her workshops has done (and continues to do) for me.

Kanta is a Peaceful Warrior. Daily she fights the good fight to inspire, transform and support the ever-widening circle of people that come into contact with her. I strongly encourage anyone who has the opportunity to experience at least some of Kanta, whether it is one of her paintings, fiber art, or something as huge as one of her workshops. It will change your life."

Millicent Greason
Owner of Urban Artware, Gallery of Contemporary American Art and Fine Crafts, Co-Founder of the SEED Collective, non-profit gallery and community center, Vice President of the Downtown Arts District Association, Winston-Salem, NC

"Beauty is the essence of soul. Kanta's altars speak deeply. Her workshop inspires our own connection to this deep source."

ARE participant [and private practice therapist]

"Wonderful creative experience with lots of ideas and insights. I especially liked the small group sharing of goals, desires and support."

ARE participant

"This was a very unusual and creative presentation."

ARE participant

"In 28 years of workshops at the ARE, I have never seen one that was better or better received."

ARE staff member

Abundance Triggers, the CD

Abundance Triggers: A Journey of Self Discovery **Kanta Bosniak with Music by Joshua Bosniak**

This Guided Imagery CD is designed to gently lead you into a state of relaxation so that you may access your personal Abundance Triggers, the inner archetypal symbols that will be most helpful for you to use as reminders to stay on track for success.

Reviews

This guided imagery CD from Kanta Bosniak works on several different levels to help you focus and direct the abundance in your life. Visually, through her cover art, the symbols she has painted awaken in you the deep, unconscious associations you may have with them as well as tuning you into them in your conscious life. Kanta's art resonates with the spirit, and the spirit is moved.

Then, there is music by Joshua Bosniak, just sort of coming in waves, as if with each breath you take you are in harmony. His music is perfectly enhancing to the relaxation you are experiencing as you are drawn into a deep state of peace by Kanta's serene voice.

You'll love the feeling of utter letting go and just traveling into a blissful place as Kanta guides you to finding the treasures that will become anchors in your daily life towards your quest for abundance. It is a CD to be listened to over and over again, simply because of the perfect state of relaxation you experience.

When you are feeling anxious or overwhelmed, or just want to regain your balance, this CD will take you to a place where you will find tranquility.

Vicky Stata

Kanta Bosniak takes us from stress to bliss in a few moments with peaceful images we can continue to recall and carry with us throughout our days.

Lisa Plummer

Kanta Bosniak's Abundance Triggers is a deceptively simple journey into a profoundly helpful "creative workshop", where you will form your own unique tools for abundant living, without even trying.

First of all, she has a gift for easing the listener into a totally relaxed state, where one is then fully open and prepared for the journey. You trust her voice, which has authority, yet a gentleness, patience and empathy.

Without revealing all of what you'll find in the place she brings you to, suffice it to say that she helps you form your own tools for productive living that are custom-designed for maximum usage.

This CD is extremely helpful to anyone wanting to increase creativity, but also to those people who want to be able to relax, to write an insightful term paper, prepare for a challenging business meeting, or simply feel more comfortable in one's own skin.

Josh Bosniak's soundtrack is an added plus. Rather than relying on the hackneyed ambient music of this genre, he branches out into new terrain, at times using male voice in a soothing, yet energetic refrain. Highly recommended!

C.M. Stine

Another success from Kanta Bosniak-- a relaxing and uplifting journey to discover your own personal power. I highly recommend the Abundance Triggers CD for anyone interested in spiritual growth and purposeful, abundant living.

I was extremely excited when I learned that Kanta Bosniak was developing another guided imagery CD-- I continue to gain so much from her Lose Weight in Theta State CD and am a huge supporter of all of her work.

The name "Abundance Triggers" had me curious to see how self-hypnosis could lead me towards a more prosperous life, as well. Little did I realize at the time where I was in my own journey towards success, or what the CD could have in store for me.

Like the other CD, I received it promptly and in perfect condition. One of Kanta's beautiful mandalas graces the front cover; the imagery is robust and soulful, the art itself evoking a feeling of richness and balance.

When I pop the CD into the player and settle into a comfortable position, I am greeted by the music that serves to lead me into my state of relaxation, a unique tune of drumming and voice. On this journey, Joshua Bosniak excels at creating a fresh style of trance music that feels jubilant and uplifting while being the perfect vehicle into serenity.

When Kanta begins to speak I am immediately soothed. The blend of her voice and the music serve to take me into a deep space of relaxation where I feel safe, comfortable, and held in love. Kanta has the gift of grace, leading you deeper and deeper into calm and relaxation at a comfortable pace, making it easy to unwind into the process.

The journey that Kanta guides you on is a very unique and powerful exploration of inner landscapes, and a deep connection with our inner guidance. Kanta's rich imagery and gentle suggestions lead you to meet two individuals who assist you in finding your own unique and powerful images.

Meeting my Archetypal Child is an incredibly powerful experience for me each time I listen to this CD—she reminds me to be creative and playful, and to take time for fun and rest in my life.

My Inner Wise Woman is a strong image of a fully-realized self, inspiring me to reach my highest, wisest path and greatest potential. Together they urge me to listen to my soul's call, and assist me in finding power objects to serve as reminders of my own inner strength and my eternal connection to my higher power.

This CD has been a great gift as I move through some of the most challenging and ungrounding times of my life. Once these journeys began guiding me into my personal power, I realized how just how much of my strength had been zapped by my own choices and the effects of the world at large, and how far I'd strayed from my soul's purpose and best self.

I am on a continuing journey to reclaim abundance and success in my life, and I'm extremely grateful that Kanta is doing the work she is and compassionately supporting myself and others on their own paths.

Each time I listen to the Abundance Triggers CD I discover more about myself and the next right steps for me. The power objects that I've uncovered are priceless tools on my journey between where I am now and who I am becoming--guideposts on the road to a more abundant and successful life. As I grow and change I am always reevaluating what abundance means to me, and this is a CD that grows with you.

Unpacking these intuitive gifts help me learn more about my life's path, and Kanta's suggestions help me hone my emotional guidance system to joy and destiny.

Carly Giesen

The imagery of this guided meditation is exquisite! It is generous with a sense of inner movement and dimension and bright with nourishing, healing lights and colors. Inner tactile suggestions range from sifting grains of sparkling sand through the fingers, to the soft touch of long, yielding grasses, to the cool feel of the solid brass compelling doorknob on a very special door...

With each listen I feel as though I have entered my very own poem, accompanied by the soothing voice of a wise and smiling, entirely unobtrusive guide. Kanta Bosniak invites the listener to joyfully merge the ages and stages of self and to achieve creative potential and life goals assisted by what she calls abundance triggers. These are personal symbolic images, archetypal power objects discovered on the inside during prayer or meditation and brought back for use in outside life.

Sometimes they are represented by actual physical objects, and sometimes by mental, emotional, and spiritual constructs that point to the truth, your truth, of unending Divine love, beauty and provision.

As Kanta explains, none of these objects exert power by themselves. Rather, all are designed to trigger conscious recall of prayerful insight. They are reminders to the mind and heart of who and how you deeply are, and of the infinitely generous Source from which you and all you can ever dream to need do spring!

Kanta and Joshua Bosniak provide lulling visionary and musical company for the listener on a pleasant and expansive walk down his or her own winding inner path to personal knowledge, empowerment and sanctuary.

Who couldn't use a few inspiring souvenirs, abundance triggers, from a journey such as this! The journey of discovery offered on this CD is one way that enlightening, encouraging contact with inner self and Higher Power can become present and effective in day to day life- and very real indeed. Enjoy.

Catherine Cummings

Afterword:

Abundance Triggers, the Musical

Before I wrote this book, I had a dream. The dream was in color, and it was the last dream of the night. Both indications of a teaching dream, something I should pay attention to. How could I not pay attention? It was a full-tilt, huge budget musical production, choreographed and scored Broadway style, jazzy dancing and all.

Big stars and hundreds of extras sang and danced the **Abundance Triggers** theme song, *"They're everywhere!"* They sang into the camera as they danced on city streets, frolicked in parks, and cultivated gardens.

They are everywhere. The Beloved does not only sit on your eyelids, but in your ears, on the surface of your skin, on the soles of your feet and the palms of your hands, and in your heart and mind.

Any and all things and not-things too… can lead you to the Beloved, open your heart and shift your state. Once you know this, your senses, thoughts and feelings all become your allies, and there is no going back.

This shift might be described like this: While once your nightmare was occasionally soothed by momentary dreams of happiness, you now live in a happy dream, with momentary nightmares, just for practice…sharpening your skills as the master you have now become at using Abundance Triggers.

Made in the USA
Charleston, SC
04 August 2011